DELICIOUS
BAKING

DELICIOUS
BAKING

Mary Cadogan

CONTENTS

ANOTHER BEST-SELLING VOLUME FROM HPBooks®
Publisher: Rick Bailey; Editorial Director: Elaine R. Woodard
Editor: Jeanette P. Egan; Art Director: Don Burton
Book Assembly: Leslie Sinclair
Typography: Cindy Coatsworth, Michelle Carter
Book Manufacture: Anthony B. Narducci
Recipe testing by International Cookbook Services: Barbara Bloch,
President; Rita Barrett, Director of Testing; Nancy Strada, Tester

Published by HPBooks, Inc.
P.O. Box 5367, Tucson, AZ 85703 602/888-2150
ISBN 0-89586-346-4
Library of Congress Catalog Card Number 85-68376
© 1985 HPBooks, Inc. Printed in the U.S.A.
1st Printing

Originally published as Good Home Baking
© 1983 Hennerwood Publications Limited

Cover Photo: Clockwise from left: Snickerdoodles,
Macadamia Chip Cookies, Molasses Crinkles, pages 34
Photo first appeared in *Cookies* by Natalie Hartanov Haughton, HPBooks

Introduction

The secret to becoming a good cook is to start with the basics. Mastering a few simple skills will enable you to produce a wealth of cakes, cookies, pies, pastries and breads. The recipes in this book are chosen to help you achieve perfect results every time. Most of the methods are quick ones using short-cuts whenever possible. Icings and decorations are easy to do. There are a few more elaborate cakes to make after you have tried the simpler ones. These cakes are not difficult; they often only require more steps.

Each chapter is based on a separate product, such as cookies or cakes. However, many of the methods used for one product will apply to another. Baked goods are made of several basic ingredients. The first of these is usually flour. Flour forms the structure of the baked product when the gluten it contains combines with liquid. Eggs add color, flavor and nutrients. Because air can be beaten into eggs, they can contribute to the leavening of a product. Fat makes a product more tender by separating the strands of gluten. Fat used in baking include vegetable shortening, butter, margarine and vegetable oil.

Some type of liquid is necessary in baked products. The proportion of flour and liquid determines the type of product. For example, pie crusts are made with very little liquid, but cakes contain a larger proportion. Liquids include water, milk and fruit juices. Other baking ingredients include leavening agents, such as baking powder, baking soda or yeast. Some products are leavened by steam formed during baking (for example, cream puffs), or by air beaten into egg whites or from creaming. Salt and some type of flavoring are usually added to baked products. In addition, honey, molasses, a fruit puree, nuts or raisins might be added to create a special product.

Cakes

Cakes are made by several methods depending on the type of cake and the ingredients.

One-bowl cakes, such as *Iced Orange Squares*, page 27, are made by combining all the ingredients in one bowl and beating with an electric mixer. This is a fast and easy method.

The **conventional method** of making cakes is to cream the shortening and sugar until the mixture is light and fluffy. This incorporates air into the mixture and will result in a light, fine-grained product. In addition, baking powder, and sometimes baking soda, is added for additional leavening. Sometimes the eggs are separated and the whites are beaten and folded in.

Sponge cakes do not contain baking powder for leavening. They are leavened by the air that is beaten into the eggs which are usually warmed over hot water. *Strawberry-Cream Cake*, page 16, is an example of a sponge cake. It is important to beat the eggs or eggs and sugar, depending on the recipe, until the mixture is light and fluffy. Underbeating will result in a heavy cake. It is not until you can leave a trail in the mixture when you lift the beaters that the mixture is ready to fold in the flour. Room-temperature eggs will beat to a greater volume and make a lighter cake. Fold in the flour without removing the air beaten into the egg mixture.

To fold in means to use a large metal spoon or a spatula to combine two or more ingredients, such as cake batter and beaten egg whites. Spoon the beaten egg whites onto the cake batter. To fold, bring the spatula or spoon down through egg whites and cake batter, across the bottom and back up the opposite side against bowl. Repeat until no egg-white streaks remain. Do not overfold or the air beaten into the egg whites will be lost.

Creaming, the method in which fat and sugar are beaten to a light creamy texture, forms the basis of many rich, flavorful cakes and cookies. Since it gives the best flavor, butter is often used for creamed cakes. However, margarine and vegetable shortening also produce excellent cakes. In fact, because vegetable shortening is softer and more pliable, it enables you to incorporate more air into the product for a lighter texture. Butter or margarine should be at room temperature before using. If your kitchen is cold, warm utensils in hot water and dry before using. Creaming will be much easier with warm utensils.

Cookies

There are several types of cookies—bar, dropped, rolled, molded, pressed and refrigerator cookies.

Bar cookies, made from soft dough, are quick and easy to make. Spread the dough in a baking pan. Cut baked cookies into bars to serve. Some bar cookies have more than one layer. Sometimes a rich, firm dough is pressed into the pan, and a topping is added later. *Walnut Brownies,* page 42, are an example of a bar cookie.

Dropped cookies, also made from a soft dough, are dropped by teaspoons onto a baking sheet. Use a rubber spatula or another spoon to push the dough off the spoon. *Whole-Wheat Raisin Drops,* page 36, are dropped cookies.

Refrigerator cookies are sliced cookies. The firm cookie dough is shaped into a roll, wrapped tightly and refrigerated until chilled. To bake, the chilled dough is cut into thin slices. This is a time-saver, because the cookie dough can be made ahead.

Molded cookies are other examples of cookies made from firm cookie dough. Molded cookies are pressed into cookie molds or shaped by hand. *Cinnamon Jumbles,* page 42, are molded cookies.

Pressed cookies are formed with a cookie press or pastry bag. These cookies take more time to shape than dropped or bar cookies. The dough must be soft enough to go through the cookie press or pastry bag, but firm enough to hold its shape while baking. *Coffee Kisses,* page 43, are an example of pressed cookies.

Pies & Pastries

All types of pastries are included in this chapter—flaky pie crusts, rich puff pastry, choux paste and crumb crusts. Each recipe includes detailed instructions.

Cutting in is the technique used to combine a solid fat and a flour mixture. Use a pastry blender or two knives to cut through the mixture until it resemble coarse crumbs. To achieve good results when making pie crusts, handle the dough as little as possible. Overworking results in a tough crust. The dough should be moist enough to form a ball, but it should not be sticky.

Puff pastry is time-consuming but well worth the effort. When rolling and folding the pastry, keep the corners as square as possible to form lots of airy layers. Refrigerate until chilled between rollings. A hot summer day is not the best time to make this pastry; it needs to remain cool during rolling and folding.

Choux paste is a versatile pastry that forms the base for many elegant desserts, such as *Paris Brest,* page 53. Choux paste needs a medium-high oven temperature to rise and set. For larger cream puffs, reduce the oven temperature after ten or fifteen minutes of baking to bake the pastry completely without burning.

Yeast Breads

Traditional breads, dinner rolls, sweet rolls and coffee-cakes are included in this chapter. Dried yeast has been used for the recipes as it is the most commonly available form. All recipes call for dissolving yeast and a small amount of sugar in a warm liquid and allowing it to stand until foamy. This is called **proofing.** This gives the yeast a good start before adding it to the other ingredients. It also lets you check if the yeast is active. Discard any yeast that does not start to grow during proofing. Don't waste other ingredients; start with a fresh package of yeast!

Dissolve dry yeast in liquid that is between 105F to 115F (40C to 45C). Use a thermometer until you can judge the temperature accurately. Too low a temperature will make the yeast grow slowly. High temperatures will kill it.

Yeast dough is kneaded to develop the *gluten,* the protein strands that trap the gas produced by the yeast and give the baked product its shape. Kneading can be done by hand or with a heavy-duty mixer with a dough hook.

Let your yeast dough rise in a warm, not hot, place that is free from drafts. The ideal temperature is about 80F to 85F (25C to 30C).

Quick Breads

Quick breads include muffins, corn bread, biscuits, scones and pancakes. The method used for most quick breads is the **muffin method.** In this method, all dry ingredients are added to a bowl. All liquid ingredients, such as eggs, vegetable oil or milk, are combined and added to the dry ingredients at the same time. The mixture is stirred only until the dry ingredients are moistened. Overmixing results in a heavy product. Biscuits and some other quick breads are made by the **biscuit method.** This is similar to pastry, because the fat is cut into the dry ingredients. However, more liquid is used to give a softer dough.

Freezing Baked Products

To freeze baked products, cool completely before wrapping. Wrap in foil or freezer paper, or place in plastic freezer bags or containers. Frosted cakes should be frozen before wrapping; wrap or place frozen cake in a freezer container for storing.

As a general rule, freeze unfrosted cakes, cupcakes and cookies two to four months. Freeze frosted cakes and cupcakes up to one month. Freeze baked pies up to four months. Do not freeze custard pies. Freeze baked quick breads two to three months. Freeze baked yeast breads up to four months. Unbaked batters and doughs should not be frozen over one month.

Equipment & Utensils

The equipment necessary for baking is fairly minimal. If you have a wooden spoon, a set of bowls, measuring cups, measuring spoons, a rolling pin, a pastry blender or two knives and a rubber spatula, you can make most of the recipes in this book.

An electric mixer or wire whisk will help with the heavy jobs, such as creaming and beating. A food processor is excellent for cutting fat into flour in seconds. Since the food processor works at such a high speed, be careful not to overwork the ingredients for pastry. Work in the ingredients in short bursts; check before continuing.

A few baking pans will serve for most of your baking needs. Useful pans include two deep 8-inch- or 9-inch-round cake pans; a 13" x 9" baking pan; an 11" x 7" baking pan for biscuits, corn bread and small cakes; a 9" x 5" loaf pan, and two baking sheets. Special pans and equipment can be added as needed.

Nonstick pans are a great time-saver. When lining pans, the quicker-cooking cakes need only the bottom lined. Richer cakes, such as fruitcakes which have a long cooking time, need the bottom and sides of the pans lined to help protect the cake from burning.

Coffee Layer Cake

Cake:
3/4 cup butter or margarine, room temperature
1 cup sugar
3 eggs
1-3/4 cups all-purpose flour
2 teaspoons baking powder
1/2 teaspoon salt
1 tablespoon instant coffee powder
2/3 cup warm milk

Icing:
1/4 cup butter or margarine, room temperature
2-1/2 cups sifted powdered sugar
2 tablespoons strong black coffee

1. Preheat oven to 350F (175C). Grease and flour 2 (8-inch) round cake pans.
2. To make cake, in a medium bowl, beat butter or margarine and sugar 5 to 8 minutes or until light and fluffy. Beat in eggs, 1 at a time, beating well after each addition.
3. Sift flour, baking powder and salt into a medium bowl. Dissolve coffee in milk. Add flour mixture to sugar mixture alternately with milk; beat until blended. Pour batter into prepared pans; smooth tops.
4. Bake in preheated oven 30 to 35 minutes or until a wooden pick inserted in center comes out clean. Cool in pans on a wire rack 5 minutes. Remove from pans; cool completely on wire rack.
5. To make icing, in a medium bowl, beat butter or margarine, powdered sugar and coffee until icing is smooth and a good consistency for spreading.
6. Place 1 cooled layer, bottom-side up, on a serving plate; spread with 1/2 of icing. Top with remaining layer, bottom-side down. Spread remaining icing over top of cake, swirling icing with a small spatula. Makes 6 to 8 servings.

Chocolate-Rose Cake

Cake:
3/4 cup butter or margarine, room temperature
1 cup sugar
1 teaspoon vanilla extract
3 eggs
1-1/4 cups all-purpose flour
1 teaspoon baking powder
1/2 teaspoon salt
1/3 cup milk
2 tablespoons unsweetened cocoa powder
2 tablespoons boiling water
3 to 4 drops red food coloring

Fudge Icing:
2 oz. unsweetened chocolate, coarsely chopped
1/4 cup butter or margarine
2 cups sifted powdered sugar
2 tablespoons milk

1. Preheat oven to 350F (175C). Grease and flour an 11" x 7" baking pan.
2. To make cake, in a medium bowl, beat butter or margarine and sugar 5 to 8 minutes or until light and fluffy. Beat in vanilla. Beat in eggs, 1 at a time, beating well after each addition.
3. Sift flour, baking powder and salt into a medium bowl. Add flour mixture to sugar mixture alternately with milk; beat until blended.
4. Pour 1/2 of batter into another bowl. In a small bowl, dissolve cocoa in boiling water; stir into 1/2 of batter. Tint remaining batter with red food coloring.
5. Place alternate spoonfuls of chocolate and pink batters in prepared pan. Swirl through batters with tip of a knife to create a marbled effect.
6. Bake in preheated oven 25 to 30 minutes or until a wooden pick inserted in center comes out clean. Cool in pan on a wire rack.
7. To make icing, place chocolate and butter or margarine in top of a double boiler over simmering water. Cook, stirring, until chocolate is melted. Remove top from simmering water; stir in powdered sugar and milk until icing is smooth and glossy.
8. Spread icing over cooled cake in pan, swirling icing with a small spatula. Let stand until icing is set. Cut iced cake into 24 bars; remove from pan. Makes 24 bars.

Top to bottom: Coffee Layer Cake, Chocolate-Rose Cake

Raisin Spice Cake

1/2 cup butter or margarine, room temperature
1 cup granulated sugar
1 egg
1 tablespoon grated orange peel
1-1/2 cups sifted all-purpose flour
1-1/2 teaspoons baking powder
1 teaspoon ground cinnamon
1/2 teaspoon ground allspice
1/2 teaspoon freshly grated nutmeg
1/4 teaspoon salt
2/3 cup orange juice
1 cup raisins
Powdered sugar

1. Preheat oven to 350F (175C). Grease an 8- or 9-inch-square baking pan. Line bottom of pan with waxed paper; grease paper.
2. In a medium bowl, beat butter or margarine and granulated sugar 8 to 10 minutes or until light and fluffy. Beat in egg and orange peel until blended.
3. Sift flour, baking powder, cinnamon, allspice, nutmeg and salt into a medium bowl. Add flour mixture to sugar mixture alternately with orange juice; beat until blended. Fold in raisins. Pour into prepared pan; smooth top.
4. Bake in preheated oven 35 to 40 minutes or until a wooden pick inserted in center comes out clean. Cool in pan on a wire rack 10 minutes. Remove from pan; cool completely on wire rack.
5. Place cake on a serving plate. Sift powdered sugar over top of cake immediately before serving. Makes 9 servings.

Left to right: Citrus Sunshine Cake, Vanilla Ring Cake

Citrus Sunshine Cake

Cake:
2/3 cup butter or margarine, room temperature
1-1/3 cups sugar
3 eggs
1/4 cup lemon juice
1 tablespoon grated lemon peel
2 teaspoons grated orange peel
2 cups all-purpose flour
2-1/2 teaspoons baking powder
3/4 teaspoon salt
1/2 cup milk

Frosting:
6 tablespoons butter or margarine, room temperature
4 cups sifted powdered sugar
3 to 4 tablespoons orange juice
1 teaspoon grated orange peel
Few drops red and yellow food coloring

To decorate:
Sugar-coated orange and lemon jelly slices

---

1. Preheat oven to 350F (175C). Grease and flour 2 (8- or 9-inch) round cake pans.
2. To make cake, in a medium bowl, beat butter or margarine and sugar 5 to 8 minutes or until light and fluffy. Beat in eggs, 1 at a time, beating well after each addition. Beat in lemon juice, lemon peel and orange peel until blended.
3. Sift flour, baking powder and salt into a medium bowl. Add flour mixture to sugar mixture alternately with milk; beat until blended. Pour batter into prepared pans; smooth tops.
4. Bake in preheated oven 35 to 40 minutes or until a wooden pick inserted in center comes out clean. Cool in pans on a wire rack 5 minutes. Remove from pans; cool completely on wire rack.
5. To make frosting, in a medium bowl, beat butter or margarine until creamy. Add powdered sugar, 3 tablespoons orange juice and orange peel; beat until frosting is smooth and a good consistency for spreading, adding more orange juice if necessary. Tint frosting with a few drops red and yellow food coloring.
6. Place 1 cooled cake layer, bottom-side up, on a serving plate. Spread with 1/3 of frosting. Top with second cake layer, bottom-side down. Spread remaining frosting around side and over top of cake, smoothing frosting with a small spatula. Make wavy lines on top of cake with prongs of a fork. Decorate with orange and lemon jelly slices. Makes 6 to 8 servings.

Vanilla Ring Cake

Cake:
1/2 cup butter or margarine, room temperature
1/3 cup sugar
1/4 cup mild-flavored honey
2 eggs
1 teaspoon vanilla extract
1-1/4 cups all-purpose flour
2 teaspoons baking powder
1/2 teaspoon salt

Icing:
1 cup powdered sugar, sifted
1/2 teaspoon vanilla extract
About 2 tablespoons milk
1 to 2 tablespoons chopped toasted almonds

---

1. Preheat oven to 350F (175C). Grease and flour an 8- or 9-inch (5-1/2- to 6-1/2-cup) ring mold.
2. To make cake, in a medium bowl, beat butter or margarine, sugar and honey 5 to 8 minutes or until light and fluffy. Beat in eggs and vanilla until blended.
3. Sift flour, baking powder and salt into a small bowl. Add to sugar mixture; beat until blended. Spread batter in prepared pan; smooth top.
4. Bake in preheated oven 25 to 30 minutes or until a wooden pick inserted in center comes out clean. Cool in pan on a wire rack 10 minutes. Remove from pan; cool completely on wire rack.
5. To make icing, in a small bowl, beat powdered sugar, vanilla and 2 tablespoons milk until smooth, adding more milk if necessary.
6. Place cooled cake on a serving plate; spoon icing over top. Sprinkle with chopped almonds. Let stand until icing is set. Makes 6 to 8 servings.

Chocolate Roll

Cake:
6 eggs, separated
3/4 cup sugar
6 oz. semisweet chocolate, melted, cooled

Filling:
1/2 pint whipping cream (1 cup)
1 teaspoon vanilla extract
2 tablespoons powdered sugar
Powdered sugar

1. Preheat oven to 350F (175C). Grease a 15" x 10" jelly-roll pan. Line pan with waxed paper.
2. To make cake, place egg yolks and sugar in a large bowl set over a pan of barely simmering water; let stand 5 minutes or until warm to the touch. Beat mixture about 6 minutes or until thickened and lemon-colored. Remove bowl from pan. Gradually beat in chocolate until thoroughly blended.
3. In a large bowl, beat egg whites until stiff but not dry. Fold beaten egg whites into chocolate mixture. Pour chocolate mixture into prepared pan. Shake pan gently to level top.
4. Bake in preheated oven 20 to 25 minutes or until top is firm to the touch. Cover cake loosely with foil. Cool in pan on a wire rack 2 hours. Run tip of a knife around inside edge of pan.
5. Sift powdered sugar over a clean towel. Invert cake onto sugared towel; remove pan. Carefully peel off lining paper. Trim edges of cake.
6. To make filling, in a medium bowl, beat cream until soft peaks form. Beat in vanilla and 2 tablespoons powdered sugar.
7. Spread whipped-cream mixture over cake to within 1/4 inch of edges. Starting from 1 short end, roll up cake, lifting towel and gently rolling up cake with aid of towel. Cake will crack while rolling. Carefully place cake, seam-side down, on a serving plate. Refrigerate until served. Sift powdered sugar over cake immediately before serving. Makes 8 to 10 servings.

1/Trim edges of cake. Spread with filling to within 1/4 inch of edges.

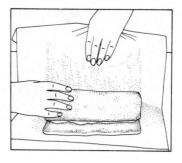

2/Starting from 1 short end, roll up cake, lifting towel and gently rolling cake.

Chocolate Roll

Simple Jelly Roll

Simple Jelly Roll

3 eggs, separated
3 tablespoons warm water
2/3 cup granulated sugar
1 teaspoon vanilla extract
3/4 cup sifted all-purpose flour
1 teaspoon baking powder
1/4 teaspoon salt
2/3 cup jam or jelly of choice
Powdered sugar

1. Preheat oven to 375F (190C). Grease a 13" x 9" baking pan. Line bottom of pan with waxed paper; grease paper.
2. In a medium bowl, beat egg yolks and warm water until foamy. Beat in sugar and vanilla; beat until mixture is thickened and lemon-colored.
3. Sift flour, baking powder and salt over egg-yolk mixture, folding in while sifting.
4. In a medium bowl, beat egg whites until stiff but not dry. Fold beaten egg whites into egg-yolk mixture. Spread mixture evenly in prepared pan; smooth top.
5. Bake in preheated oven 20 to 25 minutes or until center springs back when lightly pressed.

6. Sift powdered sugar over a clean towel. Invert cake onto sugared towel; remove pan. Carefully peel off lining paper. Trim edges of cake. Starting from 1 short end, roll up cake in towel. Cool rolled cake completely on a wire rack.
7. Unroll cake; spread jam or jelly over cake. Reroll cake without towel; place, seam-side down, on a serving plate. Sift powdered sugar over filled roll, if desired. Makes 8 servings.

Variations
Chocolate Cream Roll: Substitute 1/2 cup sifted all-purpose flour and 1/4 cup unsweetened cocoa powder for 3/4 sifted all-purpose flour. Prepare and bake as directed above. Fill with 1-1/2 cups sweetened whipped cream. Refrigerate until served.
Orange Roll: Omit vanilla. Add grated peel of 1 orange to cake mixture. Prepare and bake as directed above. To make filling, in a medium bowl, combine 1/2 cup butter or margarine, 2 cups sifted powdered sugar, 2 teaspoons grated orange peel and about 2 tablespoons orange juice. Beat until smooth. Spread 1/2 of filling over cake; roll up as directed above. Spread remaining filling over top.

Devil's Food Cake

Cake:
1/2 cup unsweetened cocoa powder
3/4 cup boiling water
3/4 cup butter or margarine, room temperature
1-1/4 cups sugar
4 eggs
1 teaspoon vanilla extract
2 cups all-purpose flour
1-1/4 teaspoons baking soda
1/2 teaspoon salt

Frosting:
1/2 cup butter or margarine, room temperature
4 cups powdered sugar, sifted
4 oz. unsweetened chocolate, melted, cooled
3 to 4 tablespoons milk or half and half
2 teaspoons vanilla extract

1. Preheat oven to 350F (175C). Grease and flour 2 (8-inch) round cake pans.
2. To make cake, in a medium bowl, stir cocoa into boiling water until completely dissolved. Let cool.
3. Using an electric mixer, beat in butter or margarine, sugar, eggs, vanilla, flour, baking soda and salt. Beat at low speed about 1 minute or until blended. Increase speed to high; beat 3 minutes, scraping down side of bowl occasionally. Pour batter into prepared pans; smooth tops.
4. Bake in preheated oven 30 to 35 minutes or until a wooden pick inserted in center comes out clean. Cool in pans on a wire rack 5 minutes. Remove from pans; cool completely on wire rack.
5. To make frosting, in a medium bowl, beat butter or margarine until creamy. Gradually beat in powdered sugar, chocolate, milk or half and half and vanilla. Beat until frosting is smooth and a good consistency for spreading.
6. Place 1 cooled layer, bottom-side up, on a serving plate; spread with a thin layer of frosting. Top with remaining layer, bottom-side down. Spread remaining frosting around side and over top of cake, swirling frosting with a small spatula. Makes 6 to 8 servings.

Easy Orange Layer Cake

Cake:
1/2 cup butter or margarine, room temperature
1-1/4 cups sugar
3 eggs
Grated peel of 1 orange
2 cups all-purpose flour
1 tablespoon baking powder
1/2 teaspoon salt
1/2 cup milk
1/2 cup orange juice

Filling & Topping:
2 seedless oranges
1 cup ricotta or small-curd cottage cheese
1/4 cup granulated sugar
1/4 teaspoon almond extract
Superfine sugar

1. Preheat oven to 350F (175C). Grease and flour 2 (8-inch) round cake pans.
2. To make cake, in a medium bowl, beat butter or margarine and sugar 5 to 8 minutes or until light and fluffy. Beat in eggs and orange peel until blended.
3. Sift flour, baking powder and salt into a medium bowl. Add flour mixture to sugar mixture alternately with milk and orange juice; beat until blended. Pour batter into prepared pans; smooth tops.
4. Bake in preheated oven 30 to 35 minutes or until a wooden pick inserted in center comes out clean. Cool in pans on a wire rack 5 minutes. Remove from pans; cool completely on wire rack.
5. To make filling and topping, peel oranges, removing bitter white pith. Cut 1 orange into sections; set aside for decoration. Chop remaining orange; set aside.
6. In a blender or food processor fitted with a steel blade, process ricotta cheese or cottage cheese, granulated sugar and almond extract until smooth. Pour into a bowl. Fold in chopped orange.
7. Place 1 cake layer, bottom-side up, on a serving plate; spread with orange-cheese filling. Top with remaining cake layer, bottom-side down. Sprinkle with superfine sugar; decorate with reserved orange sections. Refrigerate until served. Makes 6 to 8 servings.

Top to bottom: Easy Orange Layer Cake, Devil's Food Cake

Mocha & Praline Gâteau

Cake:
4 oz. semisweet chocolate
1 teaspoon instant coffee powder
1/4 cup water
5 eggs
2/3 cup sugar
1 cup cake flour, sifted

Buttercream:
1/2 cup butter or margarine, room temperature
4 oz. unsweetened chocolate, melted, cooled
2 egg yolks
4 cups powdered sugar, sifted
2 to 3 tablespoons coffee-flavored liqueur

Praline:
1/2 cup sugar
1/3 cup whole blanched almonds

To decorate:
Chocolate curls

1. Preheat oven to 350F (175C). Grease 2 (8-inch) round cake pans. Line bottoms of pans with waxed paper. Grease and flour paper and sides of pans.
2. To prepare cake, in a small heavy saucepan over low heat, heat chocolate, coffee and water; stir until chocolate melts and mixture is smooth. Let cool.
3. Place eggs in a large bowl set over a pan of barely simmering water. Let stand 5 minutes or until warm to the touch. Beat eggs until fluffy. Gradually beat in sugar; beat about 10 minutes or until mixture is thickened. Remove bowl from pan.
4. Add flour to egg mixture alternately with cooled chocolate mixture; beat until blended. Pour batter into prepared pans; smooth tops.
5. Bake in preheated oven 25 to 30 minutes or until center springs back when lightly pressed. Cool in pans on a wire rack 10 minutes. Remove from pans; peel off lining paper. Cool completely on wire rack.
6. To make buttercream, in a medium bowl, beat butter or margarine, chocolate and egg yolks until blended. Gradually beat in powdered sugar and liqueur; beat until frosting is fluffy and a good consistency for spreading. Spoon 2/3 cup frosting into a pastry bag fitted with a small star tip. Refrigerate frosting until ready to use.
7. Line a baking sheet with foil; grease foil. To make praline, place sugar in a small heavy skillet over low heat. Cook, stirring, until sugar is caramel-colored. Stir in almonds to coat. Cook until sugar is deep golden brown. Pour caramel mixture onto foil-lined baking sheet. Let stand until hard.
8. Break praline into small pieces; process in a food processor fitted with a steel blade until crushed. Or, place praline between 2 sheets of waxed paper; crush by striking with a rolling pin. Set aside.
9. Cut cooled cake layers in half horizontally. Place 1 layer on a serving plate; spread with a thin layer of buttercream. Top with another layer; spread with buttercream. Repeat with remaining layers and buttercream. Spread a thin layer of buttercream around side and over top of cake. Press crushed praline lightly around side of cake. Pipe reserved buttercream decoratively around top edge of cake; decorate with chocolate curls. Makes 6 to 8 servings.

Yogurt & Honey Cake

Cake:
4 eggs
1 cup sugar
8 oz. lemon-flavored yogurt (1 cup)
1-3/4 cups all-purpose flour
1 tablespoon baking powder
3/4 teaspoon salt
1/4 teaspoon baking soda

Topping:
1/3 cup honey
1/4 cup water
1 (3-inch) cinnamon stick
1 (2-inch) lemon-peel strip
2 to 3 tablespoons toasted sliced almonds

1. Preheat oven to 375F (190C). Grease and flour a 13" x 9" baking pan.
2. To make cake, in a large bowl, beat eggs and sugar until thick and lemon-colored. Beat in yogurt until blended.
3. Sift flour, baking powder, salt and baking soda into a medium bowl. Gradually beat flour mixture into sugar mixture, beating until barely blended. Pour batter into prepared pan; smooth top.
4. Bake in preheated oven 30 to 35 minutes or until a wooden pick inserted in center comes out clean. Cool completely in pan on a wire rack.
5. To make topping, in a small saucepan over medium heat, heat honey, water, cinnamon stick and lemon peel. Bring to a boil. Reduce heat; simmer 5 minutes, stirring occasionally.
6. With a fork or metal skewer, make holes in top of cake in pan. Remove and discard cinnamon stick and lemon peel from syrup; spoon hot syrup over top of cake. Sprinkle almonds over glazed cake; let stand until topping is set. Cut into 24 bars; remove from pan. Makes 24 bars.

Strawberry-Cream Cake

Cake:
4 eggs
3/4 cup sugar
1 teaspoon grated lemon peel
3/4 cup all-purpose flour, sifted
1/4 cup unsalted butter, melted, cooled

Filling & Decoration:
1/2 pint whipping cream (1 cup)
1 teaspoon vanilla extract
2 tablespoons powdered sugar
1 pint fresh strawberries, washed, hulled
3 tablespoons red-currant jelly, melted, cooled

1. Preheat oven to 350F (175C). Grease 2 (8-inch) round cake pans. Line bottoms of pans with waxed paper. Grease and flour paper and sides of pans.

2. To make cake, place eggs in a large bowl set over a pan of barely simmering water. Let stand 5 minutes or until warm to the touch. Beat eggs until fluffy. Gradually beat in sugar; beat about 10 minutes or until mixture is thickened and falls from beaters in glossy ribbons. Beat in lemon peel.

3. Remove bowl from pan of water. Spoon flour over egg mixture; fold in gently. Fold in butter only until streaks disappear. Pour batter into prepared pans; smooth tops.

4. Bake in preheated oven 20 to 25 minutes or until cakes spring back when lightly pressed. Cool in pans on a wire rack 5 minutes. Remove from pans; cool completely on wire rack.

5. To prepare filling, in a medium bowl, beat cream until soft peaks form. Beat in vanilla and powdered sugar. Spoon 3/4 cup whipped-cream mixture into a pastry bag fitted with a medium star tip; set aside.

6. Set aside 12 to 14 strawberries for decoration. Slice remaining strawberries; fold into remaining cream mixture.

7. Place 1 cake layer, bottom-side up, on a serving plate; spread with strawberry-cream mixture. Top with remaining cake layer, bottom-side down. Cut reserved strawberries in half. Arrange strawberries, cut-side down, on top of cake; brush with melted jelly. Pipe reserved whipped-cream mixture into rosettes around edge of cake. Refrigerate until served. Makes 6 to 8 servings.

Left to right: Mocha & Praline Gâteau, Strawberry-Cream Cake

Chocolate Ripple Cake

3/4 cup butter or margarine, room temperature
1-1/2 cups granulated sugar
4 eggs
1 teaspoon almond extract
2-1/2 cups all-purpose flour
2-1/2 teaspoons baking powder
1 teaspoon salt
1 cup milk
4 oz. semisweet chocolate, melted, cooled
1/3 cup finely ground blanched almonds
Powdered sugar

1. Preheat oven to 350F (175C). Grease and flour a 12-cup Bundt pan.
2. In a large bowl, beat butter or margarine and granulated sugar 5 to 8 minutes or until light and fluffy. Beat in eggs, 1 at a time, beating well after each addition. Beat in almond extract.
3. Sift flour, baking powder and salt into a medium bowl. Add flour mixture to sugar mixture alternately with milk; beat until thoroughly blended.
4. Pour 1/2 of batter into another bowl. Stir chocolate into 1 bowl of batter; beat until blended. Fold in ground almonds.
5. Pour 1/2 of plain batter into prepared pan. Pour 1/2 of chocolate batter in a zigzag fashion over top. Pour remaining plain batter carefully over chocolate batter. Pour remaining chocolate batter in zigzag fashion over plain batter. Gently tap bottom of pan on counter 3 or 4 times.
6. Bake in preheated oven 55 to 60 minutes or until a wooden pick inserted in center comes out clean. Cool in pan on a wire rack 10 minutes. Remove from pan; cool completely on wire rack. Place cooled cake on a serving plate; sift powdered sugar over cake immediately before serving. Makes 14 to 18 servings.

Brandy Gâteau

Cake:
1/2 cup butter or margarine, room temperature
3/4 cup sugar
3 eggs, separated
1 teaspoon brandy extract
1-1/4 cups cake flour
2 teaspoons baking powder
1/4 teaspoon salt

Topping & Filling:
1 recipe Lacy Ginger Wafers, page 40
1 pint whipping cream (2 cups)
3 tablespoons powdered sugar
3 tablespoons brandy

1. Preheat oven to 350F (175C). Grease 2 (8-inch) round cake pans. Line bottoms of pans with waxed paper. Grease and flour paper and sides of pans.
2. In a medium bowl, beat butter or margarine and sugar 5 to 8 minutes or until light and fluffy. Beat in egg yolks, 1 at a time, beating well after each addition. Beat in brandy extract.
3. Sift flour, baking powder and salt over sugar mixture; fold in.
4. In a medium bowl, beat egg whites until stiff but not dry. Fold beaten egg whites into batter. Spread batter evenly in prepared pans; smooth tops.
5. Bake in preheated oven 30 to 35 minutes or until centers spring back when lightly pressed. Cool in pans on a wire rack 5 minutes. Remove from pans; cool completely on wire rack.
6. For topping and filling, make and bake Lacy Ginger Wafers as directed on page 40. Remove 6 wafers from baking sheet immediately; roll wafers, 1 at a time, around a wooden-spoon handle to make cone shapes. Remove cones from spoon handle; cool on a wire rack. Cool remaining wafers on wire rack; break into small pieces when cool.
7. In a medium bowl, beat cream until soft peaks form. Beat in powdered sugar and brandy. Spoon about 1 cup whipped-cream mixture into a pastry bag fitted with a medium rosette tip; set aside.
8. Place 1 cake layer, bottom-side up, on a serving plate; spread with 1/3 of remaining whipped-cream mixture. Sprinkle 2 tablespoons broken wafers over cream mixture. Top with remaining cake layer, bottom-side down. Spread remaining cream mixture around side and top of cake. Press remaining broken wafers onto side of cake.
9. Pipe reserved cream mixture into wafer cones; place on top of cake like spokes of a wheel. Pipe rosettes around edge and in center. Refrigerate until served. Makes 6 to 8 servings.

Brandy Gâteau

Lemon Pound Cake

1 cup butter or margarine, room temperature
1-1/2 cups granulated sugar
6 eggs
Grated peel and juice of 2 lemons
1-1/2 cups sifted all-purpose flour
1 tablespoon baking powder
1 teaspoon salt
3/4 cup milk
Powdered sugar

1. Preheat oven to 350F (175C). Grease and flour a 12-cup Bundt pan.

2. In a large bowl, beat butter or margarine and granulated sugar 5 to 8 minutes or until light and fluffy. Beat in eggs, 1 at a time, beating well after each addition.

3. Beat in lemon peel and lemon juice until blended.

4. Sift flour, baking powder and salt into a medium bowl. Add flour mixture to sugar mixture alternately with milk; beat until blended. Pour batter into prepared pan; smooth top.

5. Bake in preheated oven 55 to 60 minutes or until a wooden pick inserted in center comes out clean. Cool in pan on a wire rack 10 minutes. Remove from pan; cool completely on wire rack.

6. Place cake on a serving plate. Sift powdered sugar over top immediately before serving. Makes 12 to 18 servings.

Orange-Meringue Gâteau

Orange-Meringue Gâteau

Cake:
2 eggs, separated
3 tablespoons orange juice
1/2 cup sugar
1 tablespoon grated orange peel
3/4 cup sifted cake flour
1/2 teaspoon baking powder
2 tablespoons sweet sherry

Meringue Layers:
2 egg whites
1/3 cup superfine sugar
1/2 teaspoon almond extract
1/2 cup ground toasted almonds
1 oz. semisweet chocolate, melted, cooled

Filling & Decoration:
1-1/2 cups whipping cream
3 to 4 tablespoons powdered sugar
1 (15-oz.) can mandarin-orange sections, drained

1. Preheat oven to 350F (175C). Grease and flour an 8-inch-round cake pan.
2. To prepare cake, in a medium bowl, beat egg yolks and orange juice until foamy. Beat in sugar until thickened and lemon-colored. Fold in grated orange peel.
3. Sift flour and baking powder over egg-yolk mixture; fold in.
4. In a medium bowl, beat egg whites until stiff but not dry. Fold beaten egg whites into egg-yolk mixture. Pour batter into prepared pan; smooth top.
5. Bake in preheated oven 25 to 30 minutes or until a wooden pick inserted in center comes out clean. Cool in pan on a wire rack 10 minutes. Remove from pan; cool completely on wire rack.
6. Place cake on a flat plate. With a fork or skewer, make holes in top of cake; sprinkle with sherry. Set aside.
7. Preheat oven to 300F (150C). To make meringue layers, line a large baking sheet with parchment paper. Draw 2 (8-inch) circles on parchment paper. In a medium bowl, beat egg whites until stiff but not dry. Gradually beat in sugar; beat until stiff and glossy. Beat in almond extract. Fold ground almonds into beaten egg whites. Spread meringue evenly over circles, keeping meringue inside of circles.
8. Bake in preheated oven 30 to 35 minutes or until layers are firm and lightly browned. Remove from oven; score 1 layer into 8 equal wedges. Cool both layers on baking sheet on a wire rack 10 minutes. Carefully remove layers from paper; cool completely on wire rack.
9. Place scored layer on a flat surface; cut into wedges. Spoon melted chocolate into a pastry bag fitted with a small plain writing tip. Pipe chocolate in a wavy line over each wedge. Set wedges aside.
10. To make filling, in a medium bowl, beat cream until soft peaks form. Beat in powdered sugar.
11. Place unscored meringue layer on a serving plate; spread with 1/3 of whipped-cream mixture. Cover with 1/2 of oranges; top with cake. Cover cake layer with 1/3 of whipped-cream mixture. Spoon remaining whipped-cream mixture into a pastry bag fitted with a medium star tip.
12. Pipe whipped-cream mixture in 8 spokes on top of cake, starting at center and working toward outer edge. Pipe whipped-cream stars around edge of cake. Reserve 1 orange section; place remaining orange sections between spokes of whipped cream.
13. Place meringue wedges along spokes of whipped cream, pressing 1 long side of wedge down slightly. Overlap wedges at cake center. Pipe a swirl of whipped-cream mixture in center; decorate swirl with reserved orange section. Refrigerate until served. Makes 8 servings.

Petits Fours

Cake:
4 eggs
3/4 cup sugar
1 teaspoon vanilla extract
3/4 cup cake flour
1/2 teaspoon salt
3 tablespoons butter, melted

Topping:
1 (12-oz.) jar apricot jam or preserves
1/4 cup water
10 oz. marzipan, tinted yellow, page 26

Icing:
1 (16-oz.) pkg. powdered sugar
1/4 cup water
3 tablespoons light corn syrup
Red, green and yellow food coloring

For decoration:
Nuts, candied cherries, small jelly candies,
  sprinkles and silver dragees

---

1. Preheat oven to 350F (175C). Grease a 13" x 9" baking pan. Line bottom of pan with waxed paper; grease paper. Dust paper and sides of pan with flour.

2. Combine eggs and sugar in a large bowl set over a pan of barely simmering water. Let stand about 5 minutes or until warm to the touch. Beat eggs and sugar about 8 minutes or until thick and lemon-colored and mixture has doubled in volume. Remove from pan; beat in vanilla.

3. Sift flour and salt over beaten egg mixture, folding in while sifting. Fold in butter only until streaks disappear. Pour batter into prepared pan; smooth top.

4. Bake in preheated oven 20 to 25 minutes or until center springs back when lightly pressed. Cool in pan on a wire rack 10 minutes. Remove from pan; peel off lining paper. Cool completely on wire rack.

5. To make topping, press apricot jam through a fine strainer into a small saucepan; stir in water. Cook, stirring, 2 to 3 minutes or until mixture is smooth. Cool slightly.

6. Roll out marzipan between 2 sheets of waxed paper to a 13" x 9" rectangle.

7. Brush top of cake with melted apricot jam. Remove 1 sheet of waxed paper from marzipan. Invert marzipan onto top of cake; peel off waxed paper. Trim edges even with cake. Cut cake into 1-1/2-inch squares, rectangles, circles or triangles.

8. To make icing, combine powdered sugar, 1/4 cup water and corn syrup in top of a double boiler set over simmering water. Cook, stirring constantly, until sugar dissolves and mixture is smooth. Divide icing into several bowls; tint with food coloring as desired.

9. Brush cut surface of cakes with apricot jam. Place coated cakes on a wire rack set over a jelly-roll pan, using a separate rack for each icing color. Spoon icing over cakes, covering marzipan and sides completely. Let stand until icing is set. Scrape up excess icing from pan; reheat if necessary. Again spoon icing over cakes. Let stand until icing is set. Decorate as desired with nuts, candied cherries, small candies, sprinkles or dragees. Makes 36 to 42 petits fours.

Double-Chocolate Cupcakes

Cupcakes:
1/2 cup butter or margarine, room temperature
3/4 cup sugar
2 eggs
1 teaspoon vanilla extract
2 oz. unsweetened chocolate, melted, cooled
1 cup all-purpose flour
1-1/2 teaspoons baking powder
1/2 teaspoon salt
1/3 cup milk

Glaze:
4 to 5 oz. semisweet chocolate
1 tablespoon shortening

1. Preheat oven to 375F (190C). Grease or line a 12-cup muffin pan with paper cupcake liners.
2. To make cupcakes, in a medium bowl, beat butter or margarine and sugar 5 to 8 minutes or until light and fluffy. Beat in eggs until blended. Beat in vanilla and chocolate until combined.
3. Sift flour, baking powder and salt into a medium bowl. Add flour mixture to sugar mixture alternately with milk; beat until blended.
4. Spoon batter into prepared muffin cups, filling cups about half full.
5. Bake in preheated oven 18 to 22 minutes or until tops spring back when lightly pressed. Cool in pan on a wire rack 5 minutes. Remove from pan; cool completely on wire rack.
6. To make glaze, in a small heavy saucepan over very low heat, melt chocolate and shortening, stirring until smooth. Cool slightly. Spoon melted chocolate mixture over top of each cooled cupcake. Let stand until chocolate is set. Makes 12 cupcakes.

Chocolate & Praline Fancies

Cake:
3 eggs
3/4 cup sugar
1 teaspoon vanilla extract
1 cup sifted cake flour
1/2 teaspoon baking powder
1/4 teaspoon salt

Hazelnut Praline:
3/4 cup sugar
3/4 cup hazelnuts

Icing:
2 tablespoons unsweetened cocoa powder
3 tablespoons hot water
1/2 cup butter or margarine, room temperature
4 cups powdered sugar, sifted
1 teaspoon vanilla extract
3 tablespoons milk

1. Preheat oven to 350F (175C). Grease an 8-inch-square baking pan. Line bottom and sides of pan with waxed paper; grease paper.
2. To make cake, in a medium bowl, beat eggs until foamy. Gradually beat in sugar; beat until mixture is thickened and lemon-colored. Beat in vanilla.
3. Sift flour, baking powder and salt into a medium bowl. Beat flour mixture into egg mixture, beating only until blended. Pour batter into prepared pan; smooth top.
4. Bake in preheated oven 30 to 35 minutes or until center springs back when lightly pressed. Cool in pan on a wire rack 5 minutes. Remove from pan, peel off lining paper. Cool completely on wire rack.
5. Line a baking sheet with foil; grease foil. To make praline, place sugar in a medium heavy skillet over low heat. Cook, stirring, until sugar is melted and caramel-colored. Stir in hazelnuts to coat. Cook until sugar is deep golden brown. Remove from heat. Grease a teaspoon; with greased teaspoon, lift out 25 nuts, 1 at a time. Place nuts at 1 end of foil-lined baking sheet. Pour remaining nut mixture onto opposite end of baking sheet. Let stand until hard. Set nuts aside for decoration.
6. Break remaining praline into small pieces; process in a food processor fitted with a steel blade until crushed. Or, place praline between 2 sheets of waxed paper; crush by striking with a rolling pin. Spread crushed praline on sheet of waxed paper; set aside.
7. To make icing, in a small bowl, dissolve cocoa in hot water; cool. In a medium bowl, combine butter or margarine, powdered sugar, vanilla, cooled cocoa mixture and 2 tablespoons milk; beat until smooth. Spoon 3/4 to 1 cup icing into a pastry bag fitted with a small star tip; set aside.
8. Beat enough remaining milk into remaining icing to make a good consistency for spreading. Cut cooled cake into 25 (1-1/2-inch) squares. Spread a thin layer of icing around sides of cake squares; roll frosted sides in crushed praline to coat. Spread a little icing on top; place squares on a serving plate. Pipe reserved icing decoratively on top of squares. Place a reserved whole hazelnut in center of each square. Makes 25 squares.

Chocolate Toffee Bars

Shortbread:
3/4 cup butter or margarine, room temperature
1/2 cup sugar
1-1/2 cups all-purpose flour

Topping:
1/2 cup butter or margarine
1/4 cup sugar
2 tablespoons light corn syrup
2/3 cup sweetened condensed milk
4 oz. semisweet chocolate
1 tablespoon shortening

1. Preheat oven to 325F (160C). Lightly grease an 8- or 9-inch square baking pan.
2. To make shortbread, in a medium bowl, beat butter or margarine and sugar 5 to 8 minutes or until light and fluffy. Stir in flour to make a smooth dough. Knead dough in bowl 8 to 10 strokes. Pat out dough evenly in bottom of greased pan. Prick dough with a fork.
3. Bake in preheated oven 35 to 40 minutes or until golden. Cool in pan on a wire rack.
4. To make topping, in a medium saucepan over low heat, combine butter or margarine, sugar, corn syrup and condensed milk. Cook, stirring, until mixture comes to a boil. Boil 5 to 7 minutes or until mixture is toffee-colored and thickened, stirring occasionally. Cool slightly. Spread over cooled shortbread in pan. Let stand until cool.
5. In a small heavy saucepan over very low heat, melt chocolate and shortening. Cook, stirring until smooth. Cool slightly. Spread chocolate over cooled toffee. Let stand until chocolate is set. Cut into bars; remove from pan. Makes 20 bars.

Clockwise from top left: Double-Chocolate Cupcakes, Chocolate & Praline Fancies, Chocolate Toffee Bars

Upside-Down Peach Cake

Topping:
1/4 cup butter or margarine
1/2 cup firmly packed light-brown sugar
1 maraschino cherry
1 (29-oz.) can peach slices, well drained

Cake:
1/3 cup butter or margarine, room temperature
1 cup sugar
1 egg
3/4 teaspoon almond extract
1-1/2 cups cake flour
2 teaspoons baking powder
1/2 teaspoon salt
2/3 cup milk

---

1. Preheat oven to 350F (175C). To make topping, place 1/4 cup butter or margarine in a 9-inch-square baking pan; place in preheated oven until butter or margarine melts. Stir in brown sugar. Place cherry in center of brown sugar mixture. Arrange peach slices in rows around cherry.
2. To make cake, in a medium bowl, beat butter or margarine and sugar 5 to 8 minutes or until light and fluffy. Beat in egg and almond extract until blended.
3. Sift flour, baking powder and salt into a medium bowl. Add flour mixture to sugar mixture alternately with milk; beat until blended. Spread batter evenly over fruit in pan.
4. Bake in preheated oven 40 to 45 minutes or until a wooden pick inserted in center comes out clean. Cool in pan on a wire rack 2 minutes.
5. Place a serving plate over pan; invert cake onto plate. Leave pan in place 2 to 3 minutes. Remove pan carefully. Serve warm. Makes 9 to 12 servings.

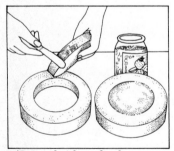

1/Spread sides of cake circles with apricot jam.

2/Flute to make a decorative border.

Marzipan-Covered Cake

Cake:
1/2 cup butter or margarine, room temperature
1-1/4 cups sugar
3 eggs
1 teaspoon vanilla extract
2 cups all-purpose flour
1 tablespoon baking powder
1/2 teaspoon salt
1 cup milk
Few drops red food coloring

Filling & Decoration:
1/2 cup apricot jam, melted, cooled
2 (7-oz.) pkgs. marzipan, tinted yellow, box below
Sugar-coated marzipan fruit, if desired

---

1. Preheat oven to 350F (175C). Grease and flour 2 (8-inch) round cake pans.
2. To make cake, in a medium bowl, beat butter or margarine, sugar, eggs, vanilla, flour, baking powder, salt and milk with electric mixer at low speed 1 minute or until blended.
3. Increase speed to high; beat 3 minutes, scraping down side of bowl occasionally. Pour 1/2 of batter into 1 prepared pan. Tint remaining batter pink with a few drops of red food coloring. Stir until thoroughly blended.
4. Pour pink batter into second prepared pan. Smooth tops.
5. Bake in preheated oven 30 to 35 minutes or until a wooden pick inserted in center comes out clean. Cool in pans on a wire rack 5 minutes. Remove from pans; cool completely on wire rack.
6. To make checkered effect, cut a 4-inch circle from center of each cake. Remove 4-inch circles. Spread sides of cake circles with apricot jam. Place plain ring on a serving plate; place pink center in plain ring. Place plain center in pink ring. See illustration opposite.
7. Spread bottom layer with apricot jam; top with remaining layer. Spread top and side of cake with apricot jam.
8. Place 1/2 of marzipan between 2 sheets of waxed paper; roll out to a 24" x 3" rectangle. Place around side of cake, extending marzipan about 1/2 inch above top edge of cake. Roll out remaining marzipan to a 9-inch circle; place on top of cake, turning edge up. Pinch edges together; flute to make a decorative border.
9. Brush bottoms of marzipan fruit with apricot jam; place around top edge of cake in a decorative pattern, if desired. Makes 8 to 10 servings.

> To tint marzipan, knead marzipan on a sheet of waxed paper until soft and pliable. Add about 8 drops of yellow food coloring for 2 (7-ounce) packages; knead until thoroughly blended.

Left to right: Marzipan-Covered Cake, Iced Orange Squares

Iced Orange Squares

Cake:
3/4 cup butter or margarine, room temperature
1-1/4 cups sugar
3 eggs
2-1/2 cups all-purpose flour
1-1/2 teaspoons baking soda
1-1/4 cups orange juice
1 tablespoon grated orange peel

Icing:
1-1/4 cups powdered sugar, sifted
3 tablespoons orange juice

1. Preheat oven to 350F (175C). Grease and flour a 13" x 9" baking pan.
2. To make cake, in large bowl, beat butter or margarine, sugar, eggs, flour, baking soda, orange juice and orange peel with an electric mixer at low speed 1 minute or until blended. Increase speed to high; beat 3 minutes, scraping down side of bowl occasionally. Pour batter into prepared pan; smooth top.
3. Bake in preheated oven 45 to 50 minutes or until a wooden pick inserted in center comes out clean. Cool in pan on a wire rack 15 minutes.
4. To make icing, in a small bowl, beat powdered sugar and orange juice until smooth. Spoon icing over top of warm cake in pan. Cool iced cake completely in pan on wire rack. Cut into squares; remove from pan. Makes 18 to 24 squares.

Simnel Cake

1 cup butter or margarine, room temperature
1 cup sugar
3 eggs
1 cup dark raisins
1 cup golden raisins
1 cup currants
1/2 cup coarsely chopped red candied cherries
1/2 cup chopped mixed candied fruit
3 tablespoons dark rum or sweet sherry
3 tablespoons orange juice
2 cups sifted all-purpose flour
1 teaspoon baking powder
1 teaspoon ground cinnamon
1 teaspoon ground allspice
2 (7-oz.) pkgs. marzipan
1 egg yolk beaten with 1 tablespoon milk for glaze

To decorate:
Sugared flowers, if desired
Ribbons, if desired

1. Preheat oven to 325F (165C). Grease an 8-inch springform pan or deep cake pan. Line bottom and side of pan with waxed paper; grease paper.
2. In a large bowl, beat butter or margarine and sugar 5 to 8 minutes or until light and fluffy. Beat in eggs, 1 at a time, beating well after each addition. Stir in raisins, currants, cherries, mixed fruit, rum or sherry and orange juice until combined.
3. Sift flour, baking powder, cinnamon and allspice over fruit mixture; fold in.
4. Place 1 package of marzipan between 2 sheets of waxed paper; roll out to an 8-inch circle.
5. Spoon 1/2 of cake batter into prepared pan. Place marzipan circle over batter. Spoon remaining cake batter over marzipan; smooth top.
6. Bake in preheated oven 2 hours 30 minutes to 3 hours or until cake center springs back when lightly pressed. Remove from oven; cool completely in pan on a wire rack.
7. Increase oven temperature to 425F (220C). Remove cooled cake from pan, peel off lining paper. Place cake on a small baking sheet. Place remaining marzipan between 2 sheets of waxed paper; roll out to an 8-inch circle. Brush top of cake with egg-yolk glaze. Place marzipan circle on top of cake; flute edge. Score marzipan in a lattice pattern with a blunt knife. Brush lightly with egg-yolk glaze.
8. Bake in preheated oven 10 to 12 minutes or until marzipan is lightly browned. Remove cake from baking sheet; cool completely on wire rack.
9. Place cake on a serving plate. Decorate with flowers and ribbons, if desired. Makes 16 to 24 servings.

Simnel Cake

Left to right: Carrot Layer Cake; Lacy Brandy Wafers,
page 40

Carrot Layer Cake

Cake:
1 cup vegetable oil
1 cup firmly packed light-brown sugar
1/2 cup granulated sugar
3 eggs
2-1/4 cups all-purpose flour
2 teaspoons baking soda
1 teaspoon ground cinnamon
1/2 teaspoon freshly grated nutmeg
1/2 teaspoon ground cloves
1/2 teaspoon salt
1-3/4 to 2 cups grated carrots (about 4 medium carrots)
3/4 cup chopped walnuts or pecans

Cream-Cheese Frosting:
1 (8-oz.) pkg. cream cheese, room temperature
2 to 3 tablespoons lemon juice
3-1/2 cups sifted powdered sugar
About 1/3 cup finely chopped walnuts or pecans

1. Preheat oven to 350F (175C). Grease and flour 2 (9-inch) round cake pans.
2. To make cake, in a large bowl, beat oil, sugars and eggs until well blended. Sift flour, baking soda, cinnamon, nutmeg, cloves and salt over sugar mixture. Beat until thoroughly blended. Fold in carrots and nuts. Pour batter into prepared pans; smooth tops.
3. Bake in preheated oven 35 to 40 minutes or until a wooden pick inserted in center comes out clean. Cool in pans on a wire rack 10 minutes. Remove from pans; cool completely on wire racks.
4. To make frosting, in a medium bowl, beat cream cheese until light and fluffy. Beat in lemon juice and powdered sugar; beat until smooth and frosting is a good consistency for spreading.
5. Place 1 cooled layer, bottom-side up, on a serving plate; spread with a thin layer of frosting. Top with remaining layer, bottom-side down. Spread remaining frosting around side and over top of cake. Sprinkle side and top edge of frosted cake with nuts. Refrigerate until served. Makes 8 to 10 servings.

Glazed Fruitcake

Cake:
3/4 cup butter or margarine, room temperature
1 cup sugar
3 eggs
1/3 cup chopped blanched almonds
1/4 cup chopped red candied cherries
1/4 cup chopped crystallized ginger
1/4 cup chopped candied pineapple
1/3 cup chopped dried apricots
1/4 cup finely ground blanched almonds
1-3/4 cups all-purpose flour
1 teaspoon baking powder

Topping:
1/4 cup apricot jam
1 tablespoon water
2 tablespoons chopped red candied cherries
2 tablespoons chopped candied orange peel
2 tablespoons chopped blanched almonds

1. Preheat oven to 300F (150C). Grease a deep 8-inch-round cake pan or springform pan. Line bottom and side of pan with waxed paper. Grease paper.
2. To make cake, in a large bowl, beat butter or margarine and sugar 5 to 8 minutes or until light and fluffy. Beat in eggs, 1 at a time, beating well after each addition.
3. Stir in chopped almonds, candied cherries, crystallized ginger, candied pineapple and dried apricots until combined. Fold in ground almonds.
4. Sift flour and baking powder over fruit mixture; fold in. Spoon into prepared pan; smooth top.
5. Bake in preheated oven 2 hours 30 minutes or until a wooden pick inserted in center comes out clean. Cool in pan on a wire rack 30 minutes. Remove from pan; peel off lining paper. Cool completely on wire rack.
6. To make topping, press apricot jam through a sieve into a small saucepan. Cook, stirring, until jam is melted. Stir in water, candied cherries, candied orange peel and almonds. Spread warm mixture over top of cooled cake. Let stand until set. Cut into wedges to serve. Makes 12 to 14 servings.

Dundee Cake

Cake:
1/2 cup butter or margarine, room temperature
1 cup firmly packed dark-brown sugar
4 eggs
Grated peel of 1 orange
Grated peel of 1 lemon
1 cup currants
1-1/2 cups dark raisins
1-1/2 cups golden raisins
1/3 cup red candied cherries, quartered
1/2 cup chopped mixed candied fruit
2 cups all-purpose flour
1 teaspoon ground allspice
1 teaspoon ground cinnamon
1/4 teaspoon ground nutmeg
1/2 teaspoon baking powder

To decorate:
Whole blanched almonds

1. Preheat oven to 325F (165C). Grease a deep 8-inch-round cake pan or springform pan. Line bottom and side of pan with waxed paper. Grease paper.
2. To make cake, in a large bowl, beat butter or margarine and brown sugar 5 to 8 minutes or until light and fluffy. Beat in eggs, 1 at a time, beating well after each addition. Fold in orange peel, lemon peel, currants, raisins, candied cherries and mixed fruit until combined.
3. Sift flour, allspice, cinnamon, nutmeg and baking powder over fruit mixture; fold in. Spoon mixture into prepared pan; smooth top. Decorate top of cake with whole almonds.
4. Bake in preheated oven 2 hours 30 minutes to 2 hours 45 minutes or until a wooden pick inserted in center comes out clean. Cool in pan on a wire rack 30 minutes. Remove from pan; peel off lining paper. Cool completely on wire rack. Wrap cooled cake in waxed paper; then wrap with foil. Store in a cool place up to 2 months. Cut into wedges to serve. Makes 12 to 14 servings.

1/To line pan side, cut parchment paper 1 inch longer than inside of pan and 2 inches higher than pan is deep. Snip bottom edge as shown.

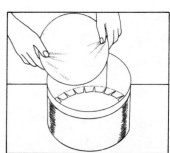

2/Place paper strip around side so snipped edge lies flat. Cut a circle to fit bottom of pan. Place circle over bottom of pan.

Clockwise from top left: Dark Fruitcake, Glazed
Fruitcake, Dundee Cake

Dark Fruitcake

1 cup butter or margarine, room temperature
1-1/4 cups firmly packed dark-brown sugar
2 eggs
1 cup currants
3/4 cup golden raisins
3/4 cup dark raisins
2-1/3 cups all-purpose flour
2 teaspoons baking powder
1 teaspoon ground cinnamon
1/2 teaspoon ground allspice
2/3 cup dark beer

1. Preheat oven to 300F (150C). Grease a deep 8-inch-round cake pan or springform pan. Line bottom and sides of pan with parchment paper, extending paper 1 inch above rim of pan. See opposite page.
2. In a large bowl, beat butter or margarine and brown sugar 5 to 8 minutes or until light and fluffy. Beat in eggs, 1 at a time, beating well after each addition. Stir in currants and raisins with a wooden spoon.
3. Sift flour, baking powder, cinnamon and allspice into a medium bowl. Add flour mixture to sugar mixture alternately with beer; stir with a wooden spoon until blended. Spoon mixture into prepared pan; smooth top.
4. Bake in preheated oven 2 hours 30 minutes or until a wooden pick inserted in center comes out clean.
5. Cool completely in pan on a wire rack. Remove from pan; peel off lining paper. Wrap cooled cake in waxed paper; then wrap with foil. Store 2 or 3 days in a cool place before serving. Cut into wedges to serve. Makes 10 to 12 servings.

Farmhouse Fruitcake

3/4 cup butter or margarine, room temperature
1 cup granulated sugar
3 eggs
2 cups raisins or currants or a combination
1/2 cup chopped mixed candied fruit
2 cups all-purpose flour
2 teaspoons baking powder
1 teaspoon ground cinnamon
1/2 teaspoon ground allspice
1/2 cup milk
Crystal sugar or crushed sugar cubes

---

1. Preheat oven to 325F (165C). Grease an 8-inch spring-form pan or deep cake pan. Line bottom and side of pan with waxed paper; grease paper.
2. In a large bowl, beat butter or margarine and granulated sugar 5 to 8 minutes or until light and fluffy. Beat in eggs. Stir in raisins or currants and mixed fruit until combined.
3. Sift flour, baking powder, cinnamon and allspice into a medium bowl. Add flour mixture to fruit mixture alternately with milk; stir until blended. Spoon mixture into prepared pan; smooth top. Sprinkle with coarse sugar.
4. Bake in preheated oven 2 hours or until a wooden pick inserted in center comes out clean. Cool in pan on a wire rack 15 minutes. Remove from pan; peel off lining paper. Cool completely on wire rack. Makes 10 to 12 servings.

Left to right: Christmas-Candle Cake, Farmhouse Fruitcake

Applesauce-Date Cake

1/4 cup butter or margarine, room temperature
1/2 cup granulated sugar
1 egg
1 teaspoon vanilla extract
1 cup applesauce
1-1/4 cups all-purpose flour
1 teaspoon baking soda
1/2 teaspoon baking powder
1/2 teaspoon ground cinnamon
1/4 teaspoon ground cloves
1/4 teaspoon freshly grated nutmeg
1 cup snipped dates
1/2 cup chopped walnuts or pecans, if desired
Powdered sugar

---

1. Preheat oven to 350F (175C). Grease and flour a 9-inch-square baking pan.
2. In a medium bowl, beat butter or margarine and sugar 5 to 8 minutes or until light and fluffy. Beat in egg and vanilla until blended. Stir in applesauce until combined.
3. Sift flour, baking soda, baking powder, cinnamon, cloves and nutmeg over applesauce mixture; fold in. Fold in dates and chopped nuts, if desired. Pour batter into prepared pan; smooth top.
4. Bake in preheated oven 25 to 30 minutes or until center springs back when lightly pressed. Cool in pan on a wire rack. Cut into squares. Sift powdered sugar over squares immediately before serving. Makes 9 servings.

Christmas-Candle Cake

Cake:
3/4 cup butter or margarine, room temperature
1 cup firmly packed light-brown sugar
4 eggs
Grated peel of 1 lemon
2 tablespoons brandy
2 cups currants
1-1/3 cups golden raisins
3/4 cup dark raisins
1/3 cup red candied cherries, halved
1/3 cup chopped mixed candied fruit
1/3 cup chopped blanched almonds
1-3/4 cups all-purpose flour
1/2 cup ground almonds
1 teaspoon ground cinnamon
1/2 teaspoon freshly grated nutmeg
1/2 teaspoon ground allspice

Topping:
1/3 cup apricot jam, melted, cooled
2 (7-oz.) pkgs. marzipan

Icing:
3 egg whites
1/2 teaspoon cream of tartar
1 (16-oz.) pkg. powdered sugar, sifted

To decorate:
1 (7-oz.) pkg. marzipan
Red, yellow and green food coloring

1. Preheat oven to 325F (165C). Grease an 8-inch spring-form pan or deep cake pan. Line bottom and side of pan with waxed paper; grease paper.
2. To make cake, in a large bowl, beat butter or margarine and brown sugar 5 to 8 minutes or until light and fluffy. Beat in eggs and lemon peel; beat until blended. Beat in brandy.
3. Stir in currants, raisins, candied cherries, mixed fruit and chopped almonds until combined. Sift flour, ground almonds, cinnamon, nutmeg and allspice over fruit mixture; stir with a wooden spoon until combined. Spoon mixture into prepared pan; smooth top.
4. Bake in preheated oven 3 hours to 3 hours 30 minutes or until a wooden pick inserted in center comes out clean. Cool completely in pan on a wire rack. Remove from pan; peel off lining paper. Wrap in waxed paper. Overwrap in foil; store in airtight container in a cool place at least 1 month before serving.
5. When ready to serve, brush top and side of cake with melted jam. Roll out 1 package of marzipan between 2 sheets of waxed paper to a 9-inch circle. Center marzipan circle on top of cake; press edges of marzipan on side of cake. Roll out second package of marzipan to a strip 25 inches long and about 2 inches wide. Brush strip with jam, wrap around side of cake, jam-side in. Press edges of marzipan around top edge of cake to make a smooth edge. Place cake on a serving plate.
6. To make icing, in a large bowl, beat egg whites and cream of tartar until soft peaks form. Gradually beat in powdered sugar. Beat until icing stands in sharp peaks when beaters are lifted. Cover bowl with a damp cloth to prevent icing from drying out while using.
7. Spread a thin layer of icing around side and over top of cake, covering marzipan completely. Let stand until icing is firm. Spread with a second layer of icing; let stand until firm. Spread with a third layer of icing, making icing as smooth as possible. Let stand until icing is completely dry.
8. To decorate, divide package of marzipan into small pieces. Tint some pieces red, some green and 1 small piece yellow, page 26. Roll out each tinted piece of marzipan separately between 2 sheets of waxed paper. Cut candle from red marzipan; brush 1 side with melted jam. Starting about 1-1/2 inches from edge of cake, place candle in center, jam-side down. Use remaining red marzipan to make holly berries.
9. Cut holly leaves from green marzipan; brush 1 side with jam; arrange decoratively on top of cake, jam-side down. Decorate leaves with red holly berries. Roll out yellow marzipan; shape into a flame for candle. Brush 1 side with melted jam; attach to top of candle, jam-side down. Tie red and green ribbons around cake, if desired. Makes 16 to 24 servings.

Molasses Crinkles

3/4 cup butter or margarine, room temperature
1 cup sugar
1/4 cup molasses
1 egg
2-1/4 cups all-purpose flour
2 teaspoons baking soda
1-1/2 teaspoons ground ginger
1 teaspoon ground cinnamon
1/2 teaspoon ground cloves
1/2 teaspoon salt
Sugar

1. Preheat oven to 375F (190C). Grease 2 baking sheets.
2. In a medium bowl, beat butter or margarine and 1 cup sugar 5 to 8 minutes or until light and fluffy. Beat in molasses and egg until blended. Sift flour, baking soda, ginger, cinnamon, cloves and salt over sugar mixture. Stir with a wooden spoon to make a stiff dough.
3. Shape dough into walnut-sized balls; roll in sugar to coat. Place about 2-1/2 inches apart on greased baking sheets.
4. Bake in preheated oven 12 to 14 minutes. Remove from baking sheets; cool on wire racks. Makes about 30 cookies.

Variation
Add 1-1/2 cups chopped raisins to cookie dough. Shape and bake as directed above. Makes about 36 cookies.

Macadamia-Chip Cookies

1/2 cup butter or margarine, room temperature
1/2 cup granulated sugar
1/2 cup firmly packed light-brown sugar
1 tablespoon light or dark corn syrup
1 egg
1 teaspoon vanilla extract
1-1/4 cups all-purpose flour
1/2 teaspoon baking soda
1/2 teaspoon salt
1 cup semisweet chocolate pieces
1/2 cup coarsely chopped macadamia nuts

1. Preheat oven to 375F (190C). Lightly grease 2 or 3 baking sheets.
2. In a medium bowl, beat butter or margarine and sugars 5 to 8 minutes or until light and fluffy. Beat in corn syrup, egg and vanilla until blended.
3. In a small bowl, combine flour, baking soda and salt. Add to sugar mixture; stir with a wooden spoon until blended. Stir in chocolate pieces and nuts.
4. Drop mixture by rounded teaspoons about 1-1/2 inches apart on greased baking sheets.
5. Bake in preheated oven 9 to 11 minutes or until golden brown. Remove from baking sheets; cool on wire racks. Makes 36 to 42 cookies.

Snickerdoodles

1/2 cup butter or margarine, room temperature
3/4 cup sugar
1 egg
1 teaspoon vanilla extract
1-1/2 cups all-purpose flour
1 teaspoon baking powder
1/2 teaspoon baking soda
1/4 teaspoon salt
2 teaspoons ground cinnamon mixed with
    2 tablespoons sugar

1. Preheat oven to 375F (190C).
2. In a medium bowl, beat butter or margarine and sugar 5 to 8 minutes or until light and fluffy. Beat in egg and vanilla until blended.
3. Sift flour, baking powder, baking soda and salt over sugar mixture. Stir with a wooden spoon to make a stiff dough.
4. Shape dough into walnut-sized balls; roll in cinnamon-sugar mixture to coat. Place balls about 2 inches apart on ungreased baking sheets.
5. Bake in preheated oven 10 to 12 minutes or until lightly browned. Remove from baking sheets; cool on wire racks. Makes about 36 cookies.

Clockwise from center left: Snickerdoodles, Macadamia-Chip Cookies, Molasses Crinkles

Whole-Wheat Raisin Drops

1 cup whole-wheat flour
1 cup all-purpose flour
1 teaspoon baking powder
1/2 teaspoon salt
1/2 teaspoon ground cinnamon
1/4 teaspoon freshly grated nutmeg
3/4 cup butter or margarine, room temperature
1 cup sugar
2 eggs
1 cup raisins

1. Preheat oven to 375F (190C). Grease 2 baking sheets.
2. In a small bowl, combine flours, baking powder, salt, cinnamon and nutmeg; set aside.
3. In a medium bowl, beat butter or margarine and sugar 5 to 8 minutes or until light and fluffy. Beat in eggs until blended. Add flour mixture; stir with a wooden spoon until combined. Stir in raisins.
4. Drop mixture by rounded teaspoons about 1-1/2 inches apart on greased baking sheets.
5. Bake in preheated oven 12 to 15 minutes or until golden brown. Remove from baking sheets; cool on wire racks. Makes about 36 cookies.

Crunchy Peanut Cookies

1/2 cup butter or margarine, room temperature
3/4 cup firmly packed light-brown sugar
1/2 cup granulated sugar
2 eggs
1/2 cup crunchy peanut butter
1-3/4 cups all-purpose flour
1/2 teaspoon baking powder
1/2 teaspoon baking soda
1/2 teaspoon salt

1. In a medium bowl, beat butter or margarine and sugars 5 to 8 minutes or until light and fluffy. Beat in eggs and peanut butter until blended.
2. Sift flour, baking powder, baking soda and salt over peanut-butter mixture; stir with a wooden spoon until blended. Cover bowl with plastic wrap; refrigerate 1 hour.
3. Preheat oven to 375F (190C). Grease 2 or 3 baking sheets.
4. Shape dough into 1-inch balls; place about 1-1/2 inches apart on greased baking sheets. Flatten each ball in a crisscross pattern with prongs of a fork dipped in sugar.
5. Bake in preheated oven 10 to 12 minutes or until golden brown. Remove from baking sheets; cool on wire racks. Makes about 48 cookies.

Variation
Stir in 1/2 cup finely chopped peanuts with flour mixture.

Left to right: Whole-Wheat Raisin Drops, Crunchy Peanut Cookies, Shortbread, Hazelnut-Chip Cookies

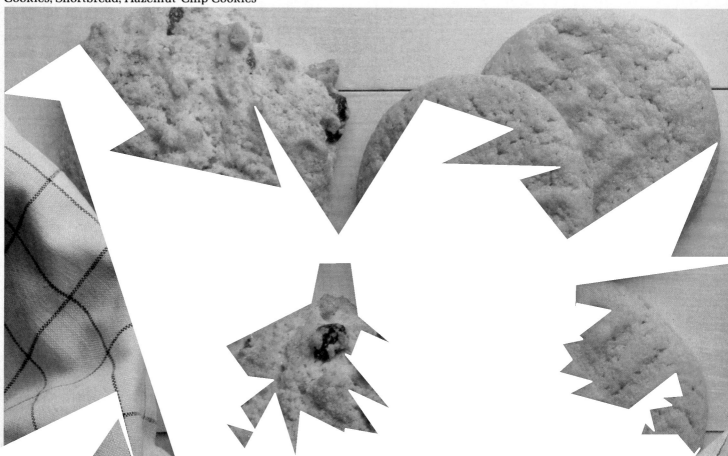

Shortbread

1/2 cup butter or margarine, room temperature
1/3 cup superfine sugar
1/4 cup ground blanched almonds
1/4 cup finely chopped candied orange peel
   or lemon peel
1-1/4 cups all-purpose flour
About 2 tablespoons granulated sugar

---

1. Preheat oven to 325F (165C). Grease a 9- or 10-inch fluted quiche pan or tart pan with a removable bottom.
2. In a medium bowl, beat butter or margarine and superfine sugar 5 to 8 minutes or until light and fluffy. Stir in almonds and candied peel. Add flour; stir with a wooden spoon to make a soft dough. Knead dough in bowl 8 to 10 strokes.
3. Pat out dough evenly in bottom of greased pan, carefully pressing dough into fluted ridges. Smooth top of dough with back of a spoon; prick with a fork.
4. Bake in preheated oven 30 to 35 minutes or until golden. Cool in pan on a wire rack 10 minutes. Sprinkle with granulated sugar. Remove from pan; cool completely on wire rack. Cut into 8 to 10 wedges. Makes 8 to 10 cookies.

Hazelnut-Chip Cookies

1/2 cup butter or margarine, room temperature
3/4 cup firmly packed light-brown sugar
2 tablespoons molasses
1 egg
2 cups all-purpose flour
1 teaspoon baking powder
1 teaspoon ground cinnamon
1/3 cup finely chopped toasted hazelnuts or almonds
1 oz. semisweet chocolate, chopped

---

1. In a medium bowl, beat butter or margarine and brown sugar 5 to 8 minutes or until light and fluffy. Beat in molasses and egg until blended.
2. In a small bowl, combine flour, baking powder and cinnamon. Add flour mixture to sugar mixture; stir with a wooden spoon until blended. Stir in nuts and chocolate.
3. Shape dough into a 2-inch-thick roll. Wrap in waxed paper or plastic wrap; refrigerate 2 to 3 hours or until firm.
4. Preheat oven to 375F (190C). Grease 2 or 3 baking sheets. Cut dough into 3/8-inch-thick slices. Place cookies about 1 inch apart on greased baking sheets.
5. Bake in preheated oven 10 to 12 minutes or until lightly browned. Remove from baking sheets; cool on wire racks. Makes 36 to 42 cookies.

Almond Macaroons

3/4 cup ground blanched almonds
1/2 cup sugar
3 egg whites
1/2 teaspoon almond extract
20 whole almonds

1. Preheat oven to 350F (175C). Line 2 baking sheets with parchment paper.
2. In a medium bowl, combine ground almonds and sugar; set aside.
3. In a medium bowl, beat egg whites until stiff but not dry. Fold beaten egg whites and almond extract into sugar mixture.
4. Spoon mixture into a pastry bag fitted with a number 6 plain tip. Pipe 20 mounds of mixture about 1-1/2 inches apart on parchment-lined baking sheets. Place 1 whole almond in center of each cookie.
5. Bake in preheated oven 20 to 25 minutes or until golden. Cool on baking sheets on wire racks 1 minute. Peel cookies off paper; cool on wire racks. Makes about 20 cookies.

Florentines

1/4 cup butter or margarine
1/3 cup firmly packed light-brown sugar
2 tablespoons light corn syrup
1/4 cup chopped red candied cherries
1/4 cup chopped walnuts, pecans, almonds or hazelnuts
1/4 cup currants
1/4 cup chopped mixed candied fruit
3 tablespoons all-purpose flour
1/3 cup sliced or slivered almonds
2 teaspoons lemon juice
4 oz. semisweet chocolate, melted, cooled

1. Preheat oven to 350F (175C). Line 2 baking sheets with foil.
2. In a small saucepan over low heat, combine butter or margarine, brown sugar and corn syrup. Cook, stirring, until butter or margarine melts and sugar dissolves. Remove from heat.
3. Stir in candied cherries, chopped nuts, currants, mixed fruit, flour, sliced or slivered almonds and lemon juice until combined.
4. Drop mixture by teaspoons about 2-1/2 inches apart on lined baking sheets. Flatten each cookie with back of a spoon.
5. Bake in preheated oven 8 to 10 minutes or until golden brown. Cool on baking sheets on wire racks 1 minute. Carefully remove cookies from foil; cool completely on wire racks.
6. Spread chocolate over flat side of cookies, making wavy lines in chocolate with a fork. Let stand until chocolate is set. Makes 18 to 24 cookies.

Top to bottom: Almond Macaroons, Florentines

Nutty Coconut-Oatmeal Cookies

1/2 cup butter or margarine
2 tablespoons light corn syrup
3 tablespoons water
1 cup all-purpose flour
3/4 cup flaked or shredded coconut
3/4 cup quick-cooking rolled oats
2/3 cup sugar
1/3 cup finely chopped walnuts, pecans or almonds
1 teaspoon baking soda

1. Preheat oven to 350F (175C). Grease 2 baking sheets.
2. In a small saucepan over low heat, combine butter or margarine, corn syrup and water. Cook, stirring, until butter or margarine melts. Let cool.
3. In a medium bowl, combine flour, coconut, rolled oats, sugar, nuts and baking soda. Stir in cooled corn-syrup mixture until combined.
4. Shape mixture into 1-inch balls; place about 2 inches apart on greased baking sheets. Flatten each ball slightly.
5. Bake in preheated oven 12 to 14 minutes or until golden brown. Cool on baking sheets on wire racks 1 minute. Remove from baking sheets; cool completely on wire racks. Makes about 36 cookies.

Muesli Bars

3 tablespoons honey
1/2 cup butter or margarine
1/3 cup firmly packed light-brown sugar
1/3 cup chopped almonds
1 cup quick-cooking rolled oats
1/3 cup flaked or shredded coconut
1/3 cup sesame seeds
4 oz. semisweet chocolate, melted, cooled, if desired

1. Preheat oven to 350F (175C). Grease an 11" x 7" baking pan.
2. In a medium saucepan over low heat, combine honey, butter or margarine and brown sugar. Cook, stirring, until butter or margarine melts and sugar dissolves. Remove pan from heat.
3. Stir in almonds, rolled oats, coconut and sesame seeds until combined. Press mixture evenly into greased pan with back of a spoon.
4. Bake in preheated oven 15 to 18 minutes or until golden. Cool in pan on a wire rack 10 minutes. Score into 18 bars. Cool completely in pan on wire rack. Cut into bars; remove from pan. Dip bars into chocolate, if desired. Let stand until chocolate is set. Makes 18 bars.

Top to bottom: Nutty Coconut-Oatmeal Cookies, Muesli Bars

Dried-Fruit Bars

1 (8-oz.) pkg. mixed dried fruit, chopped
(about 1-1/3 cups)
2/3 cup orange juice
1 cup water
1 cup all-purpose flour
3/4 cup semolina flour
1/2 cup sugar
3/4 cup butter or margarine
About 2 tablespoons sugar

1. In a medium saucepan over medium heat, combine dried fruit, orange juice and water. Bring to a boil. Reduce heat. Cover and simmer 30 minutes, stirring occasionally. Let cool.
2. Preheat oven to 375F (190C). Grease an 11" x 7" baking pan.
3. In a medium bowl, combine flours and 1/2 cup sugar. With a pastry blender or 2 knives, cut in butter or margarine until mixture resembles fine crumbs.
4. Press 1/2 of crumb mixture in bottom of greased pan. Spread cooled fruit mixture over crumb layer. Sprinkle remaining crumb mixture over fruit mixture; press down lightly with your fingertips.
5. Bake in preheated oven 30 to 35 minutes or until top is golden brown. Sprinkle top lightly with sugar. Cool completely in pan on a wire rack. Cut into bars; remove from pan. Makes 18 to 24 bars.

Lacy Ginger Wafers

1/4 cup butter or margarine
1/4 cup sugar
1/3 cup light corn syrup
2 teaspoons lemon juice
1/2 cup all-purpose flour
1 teaspoon ground ginger

1. Preheat oven to 350F (175C). Line 3 baking sheets with foil.
2. In a small saucepan over low heat, combine butter or margarine, sugar and corn syrup. Cook, stirring, until butter or margarine melts and sugar dissolves. Remove from heat.
3. Stir in lemon juice, flour and ginger until blended. Let cool.
4. Drop mixture by level teaspoons about 2-1/2 inches apart on lined baking sheets.
5. Bake, 1 sheet at a time, in preheated oven 9 to 11 minutes or until golden brown. Cool on baking sheet on a wire rack 2 to 3 minutes. Peel cookies off foil; cool on wire rack. Repeat with remaining cookies. Makes 24 to 26 cookies.

Currant & Spice Wheels

1 cup butter or margarine, room temperature
1 cup firmly packed light-brown sugar
1 egg
2-1/3 cups all-purpose flour
2 tablespoons ground almonds
1 teaspoon pumpkin-pie spice
1/2 teaspoon baking soda
1/4 cup currants
1 egg white beaten with 1 tablespoon water for glaze
1/4 cup granulated sugar

1. In a medium bowl, beat butter or margarine and brown sugar 5 to 8 minutes or until light and fluffy. Beat in egg until blended. In a medium bowl, combine flour, almonds, pumpkin-pie spice and baking soda. Add to sugar mixture; stir until combined. Stir in currants.
2. Divide dough in half. Wrap each piece of dough in waxed paper or plastic wrap; refrigerate 1 hour.
3. Preheat oven to 375F (190C). Grease 2 or 3 baking sheets. On a lightly floured surface, roll out 1 piece of dough to a 12" x 8" rectangle. Brush dough with egg-white glaze; sprinkle with 2 tablespoons granulated sugar. Cut dough into 24 (8" x 1/2") strips. Starting from short end, roll up each strip, jelly-roll style; place, cut-side down, about 1 inch apart on greased baking sheets. Flatten each cookie slightly with your fingertips. Repeat with remaining dough.
4. Bake in preheated oven 12 to 15 minutes or until golden brown. Remove from baking sheets; cool on wire racks. Makes 48 cookies.

Sticky Gingerbread Bars

2 cups all-purpose flour
1 tablespoon ground ginger
1 teaspoon ground cinnamon
1 teaspoon baking soda
1/2 teaspoon salt
1/2 cup butter or margarine
1/2 cup molasses
1/2 cup dark corn syrup
1/4 cup firmly packed dark-brown sugar
3/4 cup milk
2 eggs, beaten

1. Preheat oven to 350F (175C). Grease and flour an 8- or 9-inch-square baking pan.
2. Sift flour, ginger, cinnnamon, baking soda and salt into a medium bowl; set aside.
3. In a medium saucepan over low heat, combine butter or margarine, molasses, corn syrup, brown sugar and milk. Cook, stirring, until butter or margarine melts and sugar dissolves. Remove from heat; stir in eggs until blended.
4. Add molasses mixture to flour-spice mixture; stir until blended. Pour into prepared pan.
5. Bake in preheated oven 50 to 55 minutes or until a wooden pick inserted in center comes out clean. Cool in pan on a wire rack 15 minutes. Remove from pan; cool completely on wire rack. Cut into bars. Makes 16 bars.

Left to right: Currant & Spice Wheels, Dried-Fruit Bars

Cinnamon Jumbles

1/2 cup butter or margarine, room temperature
3/4 cup sugar
1 egg
1-1/2 cups all-purpose flour
1 teaspoon baking powder
1/2 teaspoon baking soda
1/2 teaspoon salt
1-1/4 teaspoons ground cinnamon
2 tablespoons sugar

1. In a medium bowl, beat butter or margarine and 3/4 cup sugar 5 to 8 minutes or until light and fluffy. Beat in egg until blended.
2. Sift flour, baking powder, baking soda, salt and 1/4 teaspoon cinnamon over sugar mixture. Stir with a wooden spoon until blended. Cover bowl; refrigerate 2 hours.
3. Preheat oven to 350F (175C). Grease 2 baking sheets. Divide dough into 24 walnut-sized pieces. Shape each piece into a 5- to 6-inch-long rope. Shape ropes into S shapes, circles and knots. Place about 2 inches apart on greased baking sheets.
4. In a small bowl, combine remaining cinnamon and 2 tablespoons sugar; sprinkle over cookies.
5. Bake in preheated oven 13 to 15 minutes or until golden brown. Remove from baking sheets; cool on wire racks. Makes 24 cookies.

Variation
Roll each cookie rope in cinnamon-sugar mixture before shaping.

Coffee Kisses

Cookies:
1/2 cup butter or margarine, room temperature
1/2 cup sugar
1 egg
1 teaspoon instant coffee powder
2 tablespoons warm water
1-1/2 cups all-purpose flour

Icing:
1/4 cup butter or margarine, room temperature
1 cup powdered sugar, sifted
1 tablespoon strong black coffee
Powdered sugar

1. Preheat oven to 375F (190C).
2. To make cookies, in a medium bowl, beat butter or margarine and sugar 5 to 8 minutes or until light and fluffy. Beat in egg until blended. In a small bowl, dissolve coffee in warm water. Beat coffee mixture into sugar mixture until combined. Add flour to sugar mixture; stir with a wooden spoon until blended.

Left to right: Coffee Kisses, Cinnamon Jumbles

3. Spoon dough into a pastry bag fitted with a large number 6 open-star tip. Pipe dough into small stars about 1 inch apart on ungreased baking sheets.
4. Bake in preheated oven 9 to 11 minutes or until golden. Remove from baking sheets; cool on wire racks.
5. To make icing, in a medium bowl, beat butter or margarine, powdered sugar and coffee until smooth and icing is a good spreading consistency. Mound icing over bottoms of 1/2 of cookies. Top with remaining cookies. Dust with powdered sugar immediately before serving. Makes about 16 filled cookies.

Walnut Brownies

2 oz. unsweetened chocolate, broken into pieces
1/3 cup butter or margarine
1 cup sugar
2 eggs, beaten
1 teaspoon vanilla extract
2/3 cup all-purpose flour
1/2 teaspoon baking powder
1/2 teaspoon salt
1/2 cup chopped walnuts

1. Preheat oven to 350F (175C). Grease an 8- or 9-inch-square baking pan.
2. In a medium saucepan over very low heat, combine chocolate and butter or margarine. Cook, stirring, until mixture melts. Remove pan from heat.
3. Stir in sugar until blended. Stir in eggs and vanilla until blended. In a small bowl, combine flour, baking powder and salt. Add to chocolate mixture; stir with a wooden spoon until blended. Fold in walnuts. Pour into greased pan; smooth top.
4. Bake in preheated oven 25 to 30 minutes. Cool completely in pan on a wire rack. Cut into squares; remove from pan. Makes 16 brownies.

Creamy Fruit Tart

1 recipe Quick Puff Pastry, Currant & Spice Pastries,
   page 47

Filling & Decoration:
2 tablespoons cornstarch
1/4 cup granulated sugar
1 cup milk
1 egg yolk, beaten
1 teaspoon vanilla extract
3/4 cup whipping cream
1 tablespoon powdered sugar
Strawberries, raspberries, red seedless grapes, sliced
   bananas and thinly sliced peaches
3 tablespoons apricot jam

1. Make, roll and chill pastry as directed through step 4,
page 47.
2. Preheat oven to 425F (220C).
3. On a lightly floured surface, roll out pastry to a 12" x 8"
rectangle. Fold pastry in half lengthwise. Cut a 1-inch strip
from folded pastry, cutting 1 continuous piece around 3
open edges. Do not cut along folded edge. Unfold large
piece of pastry; roll out to a 12" x 8" rectangle.
4. Place pastry rectangle on ungreased baking sheet; prick
with a fork. Brush edges lightly with water. Open the
1-inch pastry strip; place around edge of pastry rectangle.
Press edges of pastry together to seal. To flute edges, place
your fingertip on rim of pastry. Place floured knife against
pastry, pointed-end down; draw knife up against pastry
edge with quick slanting strokes. Repeat at 1/2-inch inter-
vals all the way around.
5. Bake in preheated oven 20 to 25 minutes or until golden
brown. Remove from baking sheet; cool on a wire rack.
6. To make filling, in a small saucepan, whisk cornstarch,
granulated sugar and milk until smooth. Cook over low
heat, stirring constantly, until mixture is thickened and
comes to a boil. Remove from heat. Stir 1/4 cup hot mixture into egg yolk until blended. Return mixture to
saucepan; cook, stirring, until thickened. Do not boil.
7. Pour into a large bowl; stir in vanilla. Place a piece of
waxed paper over surface of filling to prevent a skin from
forming. Cool 30 minutes. Refrigerate 2 to 3 hours.
8. In a medium bowl, beat cream until soft peaks form.
Beat in powdered sugar. Stir chilled filling until smooth.
Fold in whipped-cream mixture.
9. Spread custard-cream mixture in bottom of cooled
pastry shell. Arrange fruit over filling in diagonal rows.
10. Press apricot jam through a fine sieve into a small
saucepan. Cook over low heat, stirring, until jam is melted.
Cool slightly. Brush melted jam over fruit. Let stand until
set. Serve immediately or refrigerate until served. Cut into
slices to serve. Makes 6 to 8 servings.

Chocolate Chiffon Pie

Crust:
1 cup chocolate-cookie crumbs
1/4 cup finely chopped almonds
1/4 cup butter or margarine, melted

Filling:
1 cup milk
1 cup granulated sugar
2 eggs, separated
1/4 teaspoon salt
1 (1/4-oz.) envelope unflavored gelatin (1 tablespoon)
4 oz. unsweetened chocolate, coarsely chopped
1 teaspoon vanilla extract or 1/2 teaspoon almond
   extract
1/2 pint whipping cream (1 cup)
2 tablespoons powdered sugar

1. Preheat oven to 375F (190C). To make crust, in a small
bowl, combine cookie crumbs, almonds and butter or
margarine. Press crumb mixture over bottom and up side
of a 9-inch pie pan.
2. Bake in preheated oven 8 minutes. Cool in pan on a
wire rack.
3. To make filling, in a medium saucepan, whisk milk,
granulated sugar, egg yolks and salt until blended. Sprinkle
gelatin over milk mixture; let stand 3 minutes. Stir in
chocolate.
4. Cook over low heat, stirring constantly, until chocolate
melts and gelatin dissolves. Remove from heat; stir in
vanilla or almond extract.
5. Pour chocolate mixture into a large bowl; beat with an
electric mixer on high speed 1 to 2 minutes or until mixture is syrupy. Refrigerate 30 to 40 minutes or until almost
firm.
6. Beat chilled chocolate mixture with an electric mixer at
high speed 2 minutes or until fluffy. In a medium bowl,
beat cream until soft peaks form. Beat in powdered sugar.
Remove 1 cup whipped-cream mixture; refrigerate. Fold
remaining whipped-cream mixture into chocolate mixture.
7. In a medium bowl, beat egg whites until stiff peaks
form. Fold beaten egg whites into chocolate mixture. Pour
into cooled crust; smooth top. Refrigerate 2 to 3 hours or
until set. To serve, decorate top of pie with reserved
whipped cream. Cut into wedges to serve. Makes 6 to 8
servings.

Creamy Fruit Tart

Apricot & Raisin Envelopes

1 recipe Quick Puff Pastry, Currant & Spice Pastries,
  opposite

Filling:
1/2 cup dried apricots, coarsely chopped
1/2 cup raisins
1-1/4 cups water
1/4 cup sugar
1/3 cup ground almonds
2 tablespoons milk
Sugar

1. Prepare, roll and chill pastry as directed through step 4, opposite.
2. To make filling, in a medium saucepan, combine apricots, raisins, water and sugar. Bring to a boil over medium heat. Reduce heat. Cover and simmer 20 minutes, stirring occasionally. Remove from heat; stir in almonds. Let cool.
3. Preheat oven to 425F (220C). On a lightly floured surface, roll out chilled pastry to a 16" x 12" rectangle. Cut pastry into 12 (4-inch) squares.
4. Place 1 tablespoon filling in center of pastry squares. Brush edges of pastry lightly with water. Bring opposite corners in toward center; pinch edges to seal. Place filled envelopes, seam-side up, about 1-1/2 inches apart on ungreased baking sheets. Brush envelopes with milk; sprinkle with sugar.
5. Bake in preheated oven 20 to 25 minutes or until pastry is crisp and golden brown. Remove from baking sheets; cool on wire racks. Makes 12 pastries.

Clockwise from bottom left: Currant & Spice Pastries, Apricot & Raisin Envelopes, Mincemeat & Apple Tart

Mincemeat & Apple Tart

Pastry:
2-1/4 cups all-purpose flour
1 teaspoon salt
6 tablespoons vegetable shortening
6 tablespoons butter or margarine
1 egg
3 to 4 tablespoons iced water

Filling:
2 tart apples, peeled, cored
2 teaspoons grated orange peel
1 (16-oz.) jar prepared mincemeat (about 1-2/3 cups)
Powdered sugar

---

1. To make pastry, in a medium bowl, combine flour and salt. With a pastry blender or 2 knives, cut in shortening and butter or margarine until mixture resembles coarse crumbs. In a small bowl, beat egg and 3 tablespoons water. Sprinkle over flour mixture; toss with a fork until mixture binds together, adding more water if necessary. Shape into a flattened ball. Wrap; refrigerate 30 minutes.
2. To make filling, grate apples into a medium bowl. Stir in orange peel and mincemeat until blended.
3. Preheat oven to 400F (205C). On a lightly floured surface, roll out 2/3 of pastry to a 1/4-inch-thick rectangle. Use pastry to line an 11" x 7" baking pan; press into corners and up sides of pan. Trim pastry even with rim of pan.
4. Spread mincemeat filling evenly in bottom of pastry-lined pan. Roll out remaining 1/3 of pastry; cut into 10 (8" x 1/2") strips. Holding strips by ends, twist ends in opposite directions. Arrange twists in a lattice pattern over filling. Trim strips even with pastry rim. Dampen ends of strips; press down lightly onto pastry rim to seal.
5. Bake in preheated oven 35 to 40 minutes or until pastry is golden. Cool in pan on a wire rack. Sift powdered sugar over cooled tart. Cut into squares. Makes 8 servings.

1/Stir with end of a blunt knife to make a soft, lumpy dough.

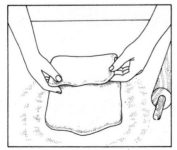
2/Fold into thirds.

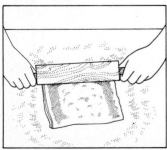
3/With a rolling pin, press edges together to seal.

Currant & Spice Pastries

Quick Puff Pastry:
1-2/3 cups all-purpose flour
1/2 teaspoon salt
3/4 cup butter, chilled
2 teaspoons lemon juice
1/2 cup iced water

Filling:
2 tablespoons butter or margarine, melted
1 cup currants
2 tablespoons finely chopped candied orange peel
   or lemon peel
1/4 cup firmly packed light-brown sugar
1 teaspoon ground cinnamon
1/2 teaspoon freshly grated nutmeg
1/2 teaspoon ground allspice
1 egg white beaten with 1 tablespoon water for glaze
Granulated sugar

---

1. To make pastry, in a medium bowl, combine flour and salt. Cut butter into small cubes; add to flour. Toss with a fork until cubes are coated. Add lemon juice and water; stir with end of a blunt knife to make a soft, lumpy dough. Do not use a fork or dough will not be the right consistency. Knead in bowl 8 to 10 strokes or until dough binds together. Shape into a 5-inch square. Wrap in plastic wrap or waxed paper; refrigerate 30 minutes. See illustration opposite.
2. On a lightly floured surface, roll out chilled dough to a 15" x 5" rectangle. Fold into thirds. With a rolling pin, press edges together to seal; see illustration. Give dough a quarter turn; roll out again to a 15" x 5" rectangle. Fold into thirds. Wrap and refrigerate 20 minutes.
3. Repeat rolling and folding dough 2 times for a total of 3 times. Wrap and refrigerate dough 20 minutes after second rolling and folding, 30 minutes after last rolling and folding.
4. Preheat oven to 425F (220C). To make filling, in a small bowl, combine butter or margarine, currants, candied peel, brown sugar, cinnamon, nutmeg and allspice. Set aside.
5. On a lightly floured surface, roll out chilled dough to 1/4 inch thick. Cut dough into 12 rounds with a floured plain 4-inch cookie cutter. Spoon a heaping tablespoon of currant mixture in center of each pastry round. Brush edges of pastry lightly with water. Gather edges of pastry; draw up to enclose filling completely. Pinch edges to seal.
6. Place filled pastry rounds, seam-side down, about 2 inches apart on ungreased baking sheets. Flatten rounds with heel of your hand. Cut 3 parallel slits in center of each pastry round. Brush tops with egg-white glaze; sprinkle with sugar.
7. Bake in preheated oven 20 to 25 minutes or until pastry is crisp and golden brown. Remove from baking sheets; cool on wire racks. Makes 12 pastries.

Pear & Hazelnut Tart

Pastry:
1 cup all-purpose flour
1/3 cup finely ground hazelnuts
2 tablespoons sugar
6 tablespoons butter or margarine
1 egg yolk
1 tablespoon iced water

Filling:
2 to 3 medium pears, peeled, cored
1/3 cup sugar
3 tablespoons all-purpose flour
1 cup milk
1 egg
1 egg yolk
3 tablespoons brandy, if desired

1. Preheat oven to 425F (220C). To make pastry, in a medium bowl, combine flour, hazelnuts and sugar. With a pastry blender or 2 knives, cut in butter or margarine until mixture resembles coarse crumbs. In a small bowl, blend egg yolk and water; sprinkle over flour mixture. Toss with a fork until mixture binds together. Shape into a flattened ball.
2. On a lightly floured surface, roll out pastry to an 11-inch circle. Use pastry to line a 9-inch quiche pan or tart pan with a removable bottom. Press pastry into fluted sides of pan. Trim pastry edge even with rim of pan.
3. To make filling, thinly slice pears. Arrange pear slices, cut-side down, in pastry-lined pan in a circular pattern. Sprinkle pears with 2 tablespoons sugar.
4. Bake in preheated oven 15 to 18 minutes or until pastry is golden and pears are lightly browned. Remove from oven. Reduce oven temperature to 375F (190C).
5. In a small bowl, whisk remaining sugar, flour, milk, egg, egg yolk and brandy, if desired, until blended. Pour over partially-baked pears. Bake 30 to 35 minutes or until center is set. Cool in pan on a wire rack. Remove from pan; serve warm or chilled. Cut into wedges to serve. Makes 6 to 8 servings.

Old-Fashioned Custard Pie

1 recipe 9-inch pastry, Apple & Orange Tart, page 55
1 tablespoon butter or margarine, room temperature

Filling:
1-1/2 cups half and half
1 cup milk
2/3 cup sugar
4 eggs
1-1/2 teaspoons vanilla extract
1/2 teaspoon salt
1/4 teaspoon freshly grated nutmeg

To decorate:
Sweetened whipped cream
Chocolate curls

1. Preheat oven to 425F (220C). Make pastry as directed through step 1, page 55. On a lightly floured surface, roll out pastry to an 11-inch circle. Use pastry to line a 9-inch pie pan. Trim pastry edge to within 1 inch beyond rim of pan. Fold edge under and flute. Brush pastry bottom and side with butter or margarine. Refrigerate while preparing filling.
2. To make filling, in a large bowl, whisk half and half, milk, sugar, eggs, vanilla, salt and nutmeg until blended.
3. Pull out center oven rack; place chilled pastry-lined pan on rack. Carefully pour custard filling into pastry shell; carefully push oven rack back into oven.
4. Bake in preheated oven 25 to 30 minutes or until filling is set. Remove from oven; cool on a wire rack. Refrigerate until served. To serve, decorate top of pie with whipped cream and shaved chocolate. Cut into wedges. Makes 6 to 8 servings.

Cherry Turnovers

Filling:
3/4 lb. fresh or thawed frozen dark sweet cherries, pitted
1/4 cup sugar
2 tablespoons water

Pastry:
1-1/3 cups all-purpose flour
1/4 teaspoon salt
1/3 cup vegetable shortening
1/3 cup butter or margarine
2 to 3 tablespoons iced water
About 2 tablespoons milk
Sugar

1. To make filling, in a small saucepan over low heat, cook cherries, sugar and water, stirring occasionally, 5 to 7 minutes or until cherries are softened. Let cool.
2. To make pastry, in a medium bowl, combine flour and salt. With a pastry blender or 2 knives, cut in shortening and butter or margarine until mixture resembles coarse crumbs. Sprinkle with 2 tablespoons water; toss with a fork until mixture binds together, adding more water if necessary. Shape into a flattened ball.
3. Preheat oven to 400F (205C). On a lightly floured surface, roll out pastry to 3/8 inch thick. Cut pastry into 12 rounds with a floured plain 3-1/2- to 4-inch cookie cutter.
4. Spoon 2 or 3 cooled cherries, without juice, in center of pastry rounds. Brush edges of pastry lightly with water. Bring edges together over filling, enclosing completely. Pinch and flute seams.
5. Place filled turnovers, seam-side up, on ungreased baking sheets. Brush with milk; sprinkle with sugar.
6. Bake in preheated oven 20 to 25 minutes or until golden brown. Remove from baking sheets; cool on wire racks. Makes 12 pastries.

Variation
Substitute 1 cup cherry pie filling for fresh cherries. Omit step 1.

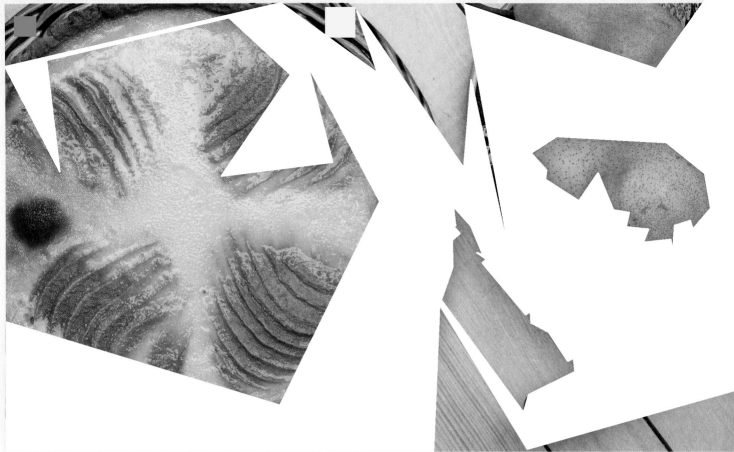

Pear & Hazelnut Tart

Lemon Meringue Pie

1 recipe 9-inch pastry, Apple & Orange Tart, page 55

Filling:
1-1/2 cups warm water
1 cup sugar
5 tablespoons cornstarch
1/4 teaspoon salt
Grated peel and juice of 2 large lemons
4 egg yolks, beaten
2 tablespoons butter or margarine

Meringue Topping:
4 egg whites
1/4 teaspoon cream of tartar
1/2 cup sugar

1. Preheat oven to 425F (220C). Make pastry as directed through step 1, page 55. Line a 9-inch pie pan with pastry. Trim pastry edge to 1 inch beyond rim of pan. Fold edge under and flute. Line pastry with foil; fill with pie weights or dried beans.

2. Bake in preheated oven 8 minutes. Remove foil and pie weights or beans. Reduce oven temperature to 375F (190C); bake 5 to 7 minutes or until pastry is golden. Cool completely in pan on a wire rack.

3. To make filling, in a medium saucepan, whisk water, sugar, cornstarch and salt until blended and smooth. Stir in lemon peel and lemon juice. Cook over low heat, stirring constantly, until mixture is thickened and comes to a boil. Remove from heat.

4. Stir 1/2 cup hot mixture into egg yolks until blended. Return mixture to saucepan; cook, stirring constantly, until mixture is thickened. Do not boil. Remove from heat; stir in butter or margarine. Pour into cooled crust; set aside.

5. Preheat oven to 400F (205C).

6. To make meringue topping, in a medium bowl, beat egg whites and cream of tartar until soft peaks form. Beat in sugar, 2 tablespoons at a time; beat until stiff peaks form. Continue beating until sugar is dissolved. Spread meringue over lemon filling to pastry edge. Do not leave any space between meringue and edge of pastry. Swirl meringue decoratively with back of a spoon.

7. Bake in preheated oven 8 to 10 minutes or until meringue is lightly browned. Cool on a wire rack. Refrigerate until served. Cut into wedges to serve. Makes 6 to 8 servings.

Cherry Basket

1 recipe Puff Pastry, Custard Mille Feuilles,
   opposite

Filling:
1-1/2 cups whipping cream
3 tablespoons powdered sugar
2 tablespoons kirsch
1 lb. fresh or thawed frozen dark sweet cherries, pitted
2 to 3 tablespoons slivered almonds

1. Make pastry as directed through step 6, opposite.
2. Preheat oven to 425F (220C).
3. Divide chilled pastry into 3 equal pieces. On a lightly floured surface, roll out each pastry piece to a 8-inch circle. Cut out 2 (4-inch) circles from centers of 2 (8-inch) circles with a floured cookie cutter. Cut 4-inch circles into 8 pastry leaves.

4. Place pastry circle, 2 pastry rings and pastry leaves on ungreased baking sheets.
5. Bake in preheated oven 15 to 18 minutes or until puffed and golden brown. Remove from baking sheets; cool on wire racks.
6. To make filling, in a medium bowl, beat cream until soft peaks form. Beat in powdered sugar and kirsch. Spoon about 3/4 cup whipped-cream mixture into a pastry bag fitted with a rosette tip; set aside.
7. Place pastry circle on a flat serving plate; spread with 1/3 of remaining whipped-cream mixture. Scatter 1/2 of cherries over whipped-cream mixture. Top with 1 pastry ring; spread with whipped-cream mixture. Set aside a few cherries for decoration. Scatter remaining cherries over whipped-cream mixture; top with remaining pastry ring. Spread remaining whipped-cream mixture over top. Sprinkle with almonds. Pipe reserved cream mixture in rosettes around top edge of pastry ring. Decorate with pastry leaves and reserved cherries.
8. Serve immediately or refrigerate up to 4 hours. Cut into wedges to serve. Makes 6 servings.

Left to right: Cherry Basket, Custard Mille Feuilles

Custard Mille Feuilles

Puff Pastry:
1-3/4 cups sifted all-purpose flour
1/2 teaspoon salt
1 cup butter
2 teaspoons lemon juice
About 1/2 cup iced water

Filling:
1/4 cup all-purpose flour
1/4 cup granulated sugar
1-1/4 cups milk
1 egg or 2 egg yolks, beaten
1 teaspoon vanilla extract
2 tablespoons butter or margarine
1/2 cup strawberry jam or raspberry jam
Powdered sugar

1. To make pastry, in a medium bowl, combine flour and salt. Cut 1/4 cup butter into small cubes; add to flour mixture. Toss with a fork until cubes are coated. Add lemon juice and water; stir with end of a blunt knife to make a soft dough. Do not use a fork or dough will not be the right consistency.

2. Knead dough on a lightly floured surface about 3 minutes or until smooth and silky. Shape dough into a 5-inch square. Wrap in waxed paper or plastic wrap; refrigerate 30 minutes.

3. Place remaining butter on a flat plate; shape into a 5" x 4" rectangle. Freeze until almost hard.

4. On a lightly floured surface, roll out chilled pastry to a 15" x 5" rectangle. Place chilled butter lengthwise on center of pastry. Fold 1/3 of pastry over butter. Fold remaining pastry over pastry-covered butter. Press edges of pastry to seal.

5. Give pastry a quarter turn; flatten slightly with a rolling pin. Roll out pastry to a 15" x 5" rectangle; fold into thirds. Wrap and refrigerate 20 minutes.

6. Roll and fold pastry 3 more times, for a total of 4 times. Wrap and refrigerate pastry 20 minutes after second and third rolling and folding, 30 minutes after last rolling and folding.

7. Preheat oven to 425F (220C). Roll out pastry to a 15" x 12" rectangle. Cut pastry into 3 (12" x 5") strips. Place pastry strips on ungreased baking sheets.

8. Bake in preheated oven 15 to 18 minutes or until puffed and golden brown. Remove from baking sheets; cool on wire racks.

9. To make filling, in a medium saucepan, whisk flour, granulated sugar and milk until smooth. Cook over low heat, stirring constantly, until mixture is thickened and comes to a boil. Remove from heat. Beat 1/4 cup hot mixture into egg or egg yolks until blended. Return to saucepan; cook, stirring, until thickened. Do not boil.

10. Pour hot filling into a medium bowl; stir in vanilla and butter or margarine. Cover surface of filling with waxed paper to prevent skin from forming. Cool 30 minutes; refrigerate until chilled.

11. Place 1 cooled pastry strip on a flat serving plate; spread with 1/2 of jam. Spread 1/2 of chilled filling over jam; top with second pastry strip. Spread with remaining jam and filling. Top with last pastry strip; sift powdered sugar over top. Refrigerate up to 4 hours. Cut into pieces to serve. Makes 6 servings.

1/Shape remaining butter into a 5" x 4" rectangle.

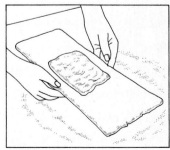

2/Place chilled butter lengthwise on center on pastry.

Beignets with Cherry Sauce

1 lb. fresh or thawed frozen dark sweet cherries, pitted
1/2 cup sugar
1/2 cup dry red wine
3 tablespoons water
2 tablespoons red-currant jelly
1 (3-inch) cinnamon stick
1 recipe Choux Paste, Cream Puffs, opposite
Vegetable oil for deep-frying
Sugar

1. In a medium saucepan over low heat, combine cherries, sugar, wine, water, jelly and cinnamon stick. Bring to a boil.
2. Reduce heat; simmer 20 minutes, stirring occasionally. Discard cinnamon stick. Let cool.
3. Make choux paste as directed in steps 2 and 3, opposite. Heat 2 to 3 inches vegetable oil in a deep-fat fryer to 350F (175C) or until a 1-inch bread cube turns golden brown in 65 seconds. Drop heaping teaspoons of dough into hot oil, a few teaspoons at a time. Deep-fry about 2 minutes or until puffed and golden. Remove with a slotted spoon; drain on paper towels. Repeat with remaining dough.
4. Place drained beignets on a serving plate; spoon cooled sauce over. Sprinkle with sugar. Makes 6 to 8 servings.

Clockwise from bottom left: Chocolate Eclairs, Beignets with Cherry Sauce, Cream Puffs

Cream Puffs

Choux Paste:
1 cup water
1/2 cup butter or margarine
2 tablespoons sugar
1/4 teaspoon salt
1 cup all-purpose flour
4 eggs

Filling & Decoration:
1/2 cup sugar
1/4 cup all-purpose flour
1/4 teaspoon salt
1-1/2 cups milk
2 eggs, beaten
1 teaspoon vanilla extract
2 tablespoons butter or margarine
2 oz. semisweet chocolate, melted, cooled
Powdered sugar

1. Preheat oven to 375F (190C). Grease 2 baking sheets.
2. To make choux paste, in a medium saucepan over medium heat, combine water, butter or margarine, sugar and salt. Bring to a boil. Add flour all at once. Stir with a wooden spoon until dough forms a ball and comes away from side of pan. Let cool slightly.
3. Beat in eggs, 1 at a time, beating well after each addition.
4. Drop dough by heaping tablespoons about 3 inches apart on greased baking sheets to make 12 mounds.
5. Bake in preheated oven 40 to 45 minutes or until puffed and golden brown.
6. Remove from baking sheets; cut a small slit in side of each cream puff to allow steam to escape. Cool completely on wire racks.
7. To make filling, in a medium saucepan, combine sugar, flour and salt. Stir in milk until mixture is smooth.
8. Cook over low heat, stirring constantly, until mixture comes to a boil and begins to thicken. Remove from heat. Stir 1/2 cup hot mixture into eggs until blended. Return mixture to saucepan. Cook, stirring, until thickened. Do not boil. Cool 5 minutes.
9. Stir in vanilla and butter or margarine. Place a sheet of waxed paper over surface of cream filling to prevent a skin from forming. Cool 30 minutes. Refrigerate 2 to 3 hours or until chilled.
10. Split puffs; remove and discard soft interiors. Spoon chilled filling into shells; press tops down lightly.
11. Spoon melted chocolate into a pastry bag fitted with a small plain writing tip. Pipe chocolate in a zigzag line over filled cream puffs. Sift powdered sugar over top immediately before serving. Makes 12 large cream puffs.

Variation
Chocolate Eclairs: Spoon choux paste into a pastry bag fitted with a large plain writing tip. Pipe dough into 4-inch lengths about 2 inches apart on greased baking sheets. Bake in preheated oven 30 to 35 minutes. Fill cooled eclairs with cream filling or sweetened whipped cream. In a small heavy saucepan over very low heat, melt 4 ounces semisweet chocolate; stir until smooth. Cool slightly. Spread melted chocolate over tops of eclairs. Let stand until chocolate is set. Makes 14 to 16 eclairs.

Paris Brest

1 recipe Choux Paste, Cream Puffs, opposite
1/3 cup slivered or sliced blanched almonds

Filling & Decoration:
1/2 pint whipping cream (1 cup)
1 teaspoon almond extract
2 tablespoons powdered sugar
Powdered sugar

1. Preheat oven to 375F (190C). Prepare choux paste as directed in steps 2 and 3, opposite.
2. Line a baking sheet with parchment paper. Draw an 8-inch circle on parchment paper. Spoon dough into a pastry bag fitted with a 3/4-inch plain writing tip. Pipe mixture into a 1-1/4-inch-wide ring inside circle on lined baking sheet. Sprinkle almonds over ring.
3. Bake in preheated oven 35 to 40 minutes or until puffed and golden brown. Remove from baking sheet; peel off paper. Cool on a wire rack.
4. To make filling, in a medium bowl, beat cream until soft peaks form. Beat in almond extract and 2 tablespoons powdered sugar.
5. Split cooled choux ring in half horizontally; remove and discard soft interior. Fill bottom of ring with whipped cream. Replace top; sift powdered sugar over filled ring. Refrigerate until served. Cut into pieces to serve. Makes 6 to 8 servings.

Crunchy Cheese Tart

Crust:
1/4 cup butter or margarine, melted
1 cup vanilla-wafer crumbs
1/4 cup finely chopped walnuts or pecans

Filling:
2 (8-oz.) pkgs. cream cheese, room temperature
1/3 cup sugar
2 eggs
2 teaspoons grated lemon peel
2 tablespoons lemon juice

To decorate:
Sliced fresh fruit, such as strawberries or kiwifruit

1. Preheat oven to 375F (190C). In a small bowl, combine butter or margarine, crumbs and nuts until blended. Press crumb mixture over bottom and up side of a 9-inch fluted quiche pan or flan pan with a removable bottom.
2. Bake in preheated oven 8 minutes. Cool in pan on a wire rack.
3. To make filling, in a medium bowl, beat cream cheese, sugar, eggs, lemon peel and lemon juice until blended. Pour cream-cheese mixture into cooled crust.
4. Bake in preheated oven 30 to 35 minutes or until filling is set. Cool in pan on a wire rack. To serve, remove from pan; place on a serving plate. Decorate top with sliced fruit. Refrigerate until served. Cut into wedges to serve. Makes 6 to 8 servings.

Clockwise from left: Crunchy Cheese Tart, Cherry Strudel, Apple & Orange Tart

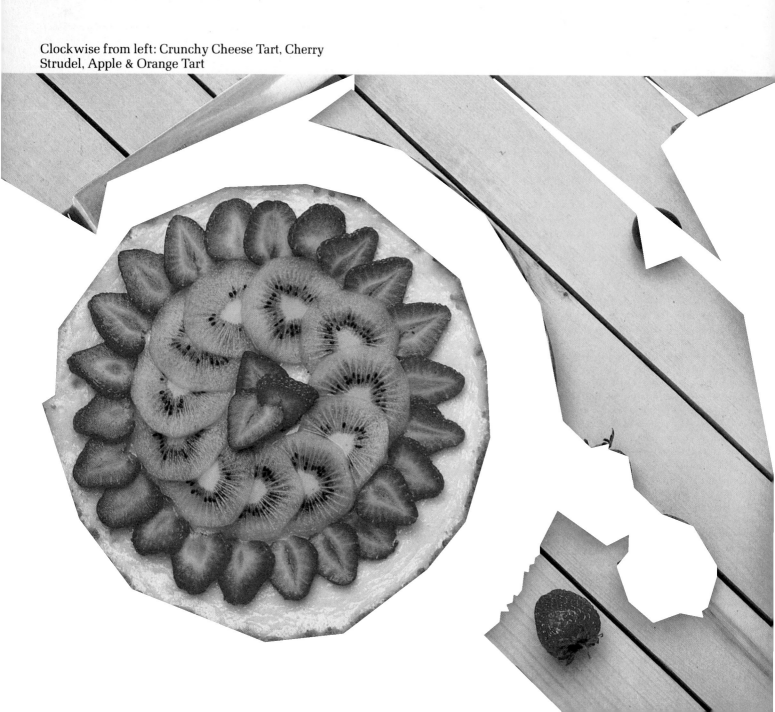

Apple & Orange Tart

Pastry:
1-1/3 cups all-purpose flour
2 tablespoons sugar
6 tablespoons butter or margarine, room temperature
1 egg, beaten
1 tablespoon iced water

Filling:
Grated peel and juice of 1 small orange
1 lb. medium, tart apples, peeled, thinly sliced
(about 3 apples)
1/4 cup sugar
2 eggs
1 cup half and half

1. To make pastry, in a medium bowl, combine flour, sugar, butter or margarine, egg and water. Beat with an electric mixer at low speed until blended. Knead dough in bowl 8 to 10 strokes or until smooth. Shape dough into a flattened ball. Wrap in plastic wrap or waxed paper; refrigerate 1 hour.
2. Preheat oven to 425F (220C). On a lightly floured surface, roll out dough to a 3/8-inch-thick circle. Use pastry to line a 10-inch fluted quiche or tart pan with a removable bottom. Trim edge even with pan. Line pastry with foil; fill with pie weights or dried beans.
3. Bake in preheated oven 10 minutes. Remove foil and pie weights or beans; let cool on a wire rack. Reduce oven temperature to 375F (190C).
4. To make filling, in a medium bowl, combine orange peel, orange juice and apple slices; toss to coat with juice. Arrange apple slices in concentric circles in bottom of cooled pastry-lined pan.
5. In a small bowl, beat sugar, eggs and half and half until blended. Pour over apples.
6. Bake in preheated oven 30 to 35 minutes or until filling is set. Cool completely in pan on a wire rack. Serve at room temperature or refrigerate until chilled. Cut into wedges to serve. Makes 8 to 10 servings.

Cherry Strudel

1/2 (1-lb.) pkg. filo dough, thawed if frozen
1/2 cup butter or margarine, melted
1/2 cup dry sponge-cake crumbs

Filling:
1 lb. fresh or thawed frozen dark sweet cherries, pitted
1/2 cup raisins
1/3 cup finely ground almonds
1/3 cup granulated sugar
1/2 teaspoon ground cinnamon
Powdered sugar

1. Preheat oven to 375F (190C). Grease a baking sheet. Unfold filo dough; place on a slightly damp towel. Cover with a second damp towel. Remove 1 filo sheet; place on a dry towel. Brush with butter or margarine; sprinkle with 1 tablespoon cake crumbs. Top with a second filo sheet; brush with butter or margarine. Sprinkle with 1 tablespoon cake crumbs. Repeat with remaining dough, butter or margarine and cake crumbs.
2. To make filling, in a medium bowl, combine cherries, raisins, almonds, granulated sugar and cinnamon. Spoon filling over filo in a 2-inch strip 1-1/2 inches in from both short ends and 1 long side.
3. Roll up strudel, jelly-roll style, starting from long side close to filling and using towel as a guide; lift and roll strudel. Tuck ends in; brush strudel with butter or margarine. Lift strudel gently with towel; place, seam-side down, on greased baking sheet, removing towel.
4. Bake in preheated oven 30 to 35 minutes or until golden brown. Cool on baking sheet on a wire rack. Sift powdered sugar over top. Serve warm or at room temperature. Cut into slices to serve. Makes 6 to 8 servings.

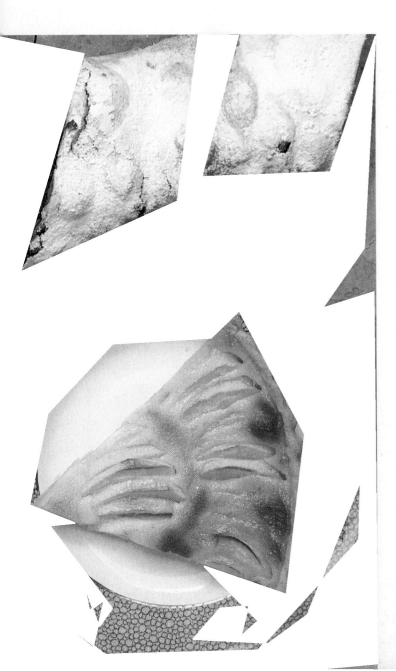

Quick Griddle Scone

2 cups self-rising flour
1/4 cup sugar
1/4 cup shortening, butter or margarine
1/2 cup currants
1 egg
6 to 8 tablespoons milk

To serve:
Butter or margarine

1. In a medium bowl, combine flour and sugar. With a pastry blender or 2 knives, cut in shortening, butter or margarine until mixture resembles coarse crumbs. Stir in currants.
2. In a small bowl, beat egg and 6 tablespoons milk until blended. Stir egg mixture into flour-currant mixture with a fork to make a soft, non-sticky, dough, adding more milk if necessary.
3. On a lightly floured surface, knead dough 8 to 10 strokes. Pat out dough to an 8-inch circle.
4. Heat a griddle or large skillet over medium heat. When hot, brush griddle or skillet with vegetable oil. Place scone on hot oiled griddle or skillet. Reduce heat; cook 10 minutes. Check bottom of scone frequently. Reduce heat again to prevent burning, if necessary. Carefully turn over scone with a large flat spatula. Cook 8 to 10 minutes or until golden brown.
5. Using spatula, slide baked scone onto a serving plate; cut into wedges. Serve warm with butter or margarine. Makes 4 to 6 servings.

Scones

2 cups sifted all-purpose flour
1 tablespoon baking powder
2 tablespoons sugar
1/2 teaspoon salt
1/4 cup shortening, butter or margarine
2 eggs
About 1/3 cup milk or half and half

To serve:
Butter or margarine

1. Preheat oven to 425F (220C). Grease 2 baking sheets.
2. In a medium bowl, combine flour, baking powder, sugar and salt. With a pastry blender or 2 knives, cut in shortening, butter or margarine until mixture resembles coarse crumbs.
3. In a small bowl, beat eggs and 1/3 cup milk or half and half until blended. Stir egg mixture into flour mixture with a fork to make a soft, non-sticky dough, adding more milk or half and half if necessary.
4. On a lightly floured surface, knead dough 8 to 10 strokes. Roll out dough to 1/2 inch thick. Cut dough with a floured 2- to 2-1/2-inch fluted biscuit cutter. Place on greased baking sheets 1-1/2 to 2 inches apart. Brush tops with milk.
5. Bake in preheated oven 12 to 15 minutes or until golden brown. Remove from baking sheets; serve warm of butter or margarine. Makes 14 to 18 scones.

Variations
Whole-Wheat Scones: Substitute whole-wheat flour for 1 cup all-purpose flour. Add 1 to 2 tablespoons more milk.
Spicy Scones: Add 2 teaspoons pumpkin-pie spice to flour mixture. Substitute brown sugar for granulated sugar.
Cheese Scones: Add 2/3 cup shredded sharp Cheddar cheese (3 ounces), 1 teaspoon dry mustard and a pinch of red (cayenne) pepper to flour mixture. Omit sugar.
Fruit Scones: Add 1/3 cup currants or raisins to flour mixture.
Yogurt & Honey Scones: Substitute plain yogurt for milk. Substitute 3 tablespoons honey for sugar. Blend eggs, yogurt and honey together; add to flour mixture. Brush dough circles with milk; sprinkle with brown sugar before baking.

Clockwise from top left: Quick Griddle Scone, Scones with variations

Honey-Nut Loaf

Banana-Raisin Bread

1/2 cup butter or margarine, room temperature
3/4 cup firmly packed light-brown sugar
2 eggs
1 teaspoon vanilla extract
1-3/4 cups all-purpose flour
1-1/2 teaspoons baking powder
1/2 teaspoon baking soda
1/2 teaspoon salt
1/4 teaspoon freshly grated nutmeg
2 large ripe bananas, mashed (about 1 cup)
1/2 cup raisins, chopped

1. Preheat oven to 350F (175C). Grease a 9" x 5" loaf pan.
2. In a medium bowl, beat butter or margarine and brown sugar 5 to 8 minutes or until light and fluffy. Beat in eggs and vanilla.
3. Sift flour, baking powder, baking soda, salt and nutmeg into a medium bowl. Stir flour mixture into egg mixture alternately with mashed bananas, stirring until combined. Fold in chopped raisins. Pour into greased pan; smooth top.
4. Bake in preheated oven 55 to 60 minutes or until a wooden pick inserted in center comes out clean.
5. Cool in pan on a wire rack 10 minutes. Remove from pan; cool completely on wire rack. Wrap in plastic wrap; store in a cool place 1 to 2 days before serving. Makes 1 loaf.

Honey-Nut Loaf

1/2 cup butter or margarine, room temperature
2/3 cup firmly packed light-brown sugar
2 eggs
1-1/2 cups all-purpose flour
2 teaspoons baking powder
2 teaspoons ground cinnamon
1/2 teaspoon salt
1/2 cup milk
1 cup finely chopped, almonds, hazelnuts,
    walnuts or pecans

For decoration:
2 tablespoons honey, warmed
Assorted whole nuts

1. Preheat oven to 350F (175C). Grease an 8" x 4" loaf pan.
2. In a medium bowl, beat butter or margarine and brown sugar 5 to 8 minutes or until light and fluffy. Add eggs; beat until blended. Sift flour, baking powder, cinnamon and salt into a medium bowl. Stir flour mixture into egg mixture alternately with milk, stirring until combined. Fold in chopped nuts. Pour batter into greased pan; smooth top.
3. Bake in preheated oven 55 to 60 minutes or until a wooden pick inserted in center comes out clean. Cool in pan on a wire rack 10 minutes. Remove from pan; cool completely on rack.
4. Brush top of bread lightly with honey. Arrange a nut cluster in center of glazed bread. Brush nuts with honey. Makes 1 loaf.

Almond-Lemon Loaf

1-1/3 cups all-purpose flour
1 cup sugar
1 teaspoon baking powder
1 teaspoon salt
1/2 teaspoon baking soda
1 tablespoon grated lemon peel
1/2 cup milk
2 eggs
1/3 cup butter or margarine, melted
2 tablespoons lemon juice
1 cup chopped almonds

Glaze:
1 cup sifted powdered sugar
1 to 2 tablespoons lemon juice
2 tablespoons sliced almonds, toasted

1. Preheat oven to 350F (175C). Grease and flour a 9" x 5" loaf pan.
2. In a large bowl, combine flour, sugar, baking powder, salt, baking soda and lemon peel.
3. In a small bowl, beat milk, eggs, butter or margarine and lemon juice until blended. Make a well in center of dry ingredients. Stir in milk mixture until dry ingredients are barely moistened. Fold in almonds. Pour mixture into prepared pan; smooth top.
4. Bake in preheated oven 50 to 60 minutes or until a wooden pick inserted in center comes out clean. Cool in pan on a wire rack 10 minutes. Remove from pan; cool completely on rack.
5. To make glaze, in a small bowl, stir powdered sugar and 1 tablespoon lemon juice until smooth, stirring in more lemon juice if necessary, to make a thin glaze. Spoon glaze over loaf; sprinkle with sliced almonds. Let stand until glaze is set. Makes 1 loaf.

Left to right: Banana-Raisin Bread; Cherry Turnovers, page 48

Coconut Bread

2 cups flaked or shredded coconut
1-3/4 cups milk
2-1/2 cups all-purpose flour
2-1/2 teaspoons baking powder
1 teaspoon ground cinnamon
1/2 teaspoon salt
1/4 teaspoon ground cloves
1-1/3 cups sugar

---

1. In a medium bowl, combine coconut and milk. Let stand at room temperature 30 minutes.
2. Preheat oven to 350F (175C). Grease a 9" x 5" loaf pan.
3. Sift flour, baking powder, cinnamon, salt and cloves into a large bowl. Stir in sugar. Make a well in center of dry ingredients. Pour in coconut mixture; stir with a wooden spoon until dry ingredients are barely moistened. Pour into greased pan; smooth top.
4. Bake in preheated oven 65 to 70 minutes or until a wooden pick inserted in center comes out clean. Cool in pan on a wire rack 10 minutes. Remove from pan; cool completely on rack. Makes 1 loaf.

Date & Lemon Loaf

3/4 cup butter or margarine
1/2 cup firmly packed light-brown sugar
1/3 cup honey
1 (8-oz.) pkg. pitted dates, chopped
3 eggs, beaten
2 teaspoons grated lemon peel
1-3/4 cups all-purpose flour
1 teaspoon baking powder
1 teaspoon baking soda
1/2 teaspoon salt

Topping:
3 tablespoons all-purpose flour
1 tablespoon sugar
1 tablespoon butter or margarine

---

1. In a medium saucepan over low heat, combine butter or margarine, brown sugar and honey. Cook, stirring, until butter or margarine melts and sugar dissolves. Remove pan from heat; stir in dates. Let cool.
2. Preheat oven to 350F (175C). Grease a 9" x 5" loaf pan.
3. Stir eggs into cooled date mixture until blended.
4. In a medium bowl, combine lemon peel, flour, baking powder, baking soda and salt. Make a well in center of dry ingredients. Pour in date mixture; stir until dry ingredients are barely moistened. Pour into greased pan; smooth top.
5. To make topping, in a small bowl, combine flour and sugar. With a pastry blender or 2 knives, cut in butter or margarine until mixture resembles fine crumbs. Sprinkle crumbs on top of batter.
6. Bake in preheated oven 50 to 55 minutes or until a wooden pick inserted in center comes out clean. Cool in pan on a wire rack 5 to 10 minutes. Remove from pan; cool completely on rack. Makes 1 loaf.

Left to right: Sticky Gingerbread Bars, page 41; Date & Lemon Loaf

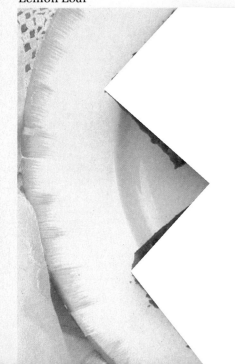
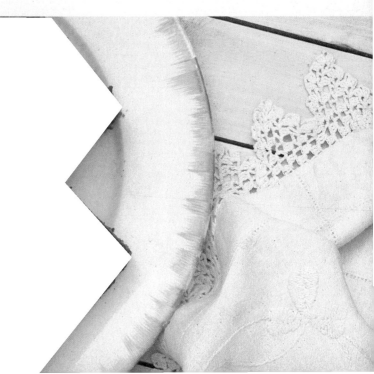

Southern Cornsticks

3/4 cup all-purpose flour
2 cups white cornmeal
1-1/2 teaspoons baking powder
1/2 teaspoon baking soda
1/2 teaspoon salt
1 teaspoon sugar
2 eggs, beaten
1/4 cup vegetable oil
2 cups buttermilk

1. Preheat oven to 450F (230C). Heat a heavy cornstick pan in preheated oven.
2. In a medium bowl, combine flour, cornmeal, baking powder, baking soda, salt and sugar.
3. In a small bowl, combine eggs, oil and buttermilk. Pour egg mixture into flour mixture; stir until dry ingredients are barely moistened.
4. Grease hot cornstick pan. Spoon batter into greased pan, filling about 2/3 full; reserve any remaining batter.
5. Bake in preheated oven about 15 minutes or until golden brown. Remove cornsticks from pan. Bake remaining batter if necessary, greasing pan again. Serve hot. Makes 12 large cornsticks.

Variation
Pour batter into a greased 8-inch round cake pan. Bake in preheated oven about 20 minutes or until golden brown.

Double Cornbread

1 cup sifted all-purpose flour
1 cup yellow cornmeal
3 tablespoons sugar
4 teaspoons baking powder
1 teaspoon salt
1 egg
1 cup milk
1/4 cup butter or margarine, melted
1 (8-oz.) can cream-style corn

To serve:
Butter or margarine

1. Preheat oven to 425F (220C). Grease an 8- or 9-inch-square baking pan.
2. In a medium bowl, combine flour, cornmeal, sugar, baking powder and salt. In a small bowl, blend egg, milk and butter or margarine.
3. Make a well in center of dry ingredients. Add egg mixture and corn. Stir until dry ingredients are barely moistened. Pour into greased pan.
4. Bake in preheated oven 20 to 25 minutes or until golden brown. Cut into squares; serve hot with butter or margarine. Makes 9 servings.

Blueberry Muffins

2 cups all-purpose flour
1/2 cup granulated sugar
2-1/2 teaspoons baking powder
2 teaspoons grated lemon peel
1/2 teaspoon salt
1/4 teaspoon freshly grated nutmeg
1/3 cup vegetable oil
1 egg
1 cup milk
1 cup fresh or thawed, frozen blueberries
Brown sugar

1. Preheat oven to 400F (205C). Grease a 12-cup muffin pan or line muffin cups with paper cupcake liners.
2. In a medium bowl, combine flour, granulated sugar, baking powder, lemon peel, salt and nutmeg. In a small bowl, blend oil, egg and milk. Make a well in center of dry ingredients; stir in egg mixture until dry ingredients are barely moistened. Fold in blueberries.
3. Spoon batter into prepared muffin cups, filling cups about two-thirds full. Sprinkle tops with brown sugar.
4. Bake in preheated oven 20 to 25 minutes or until a wooden pick inserted in center of a muffin comes out clean. Remove from pan; serve hot. Makes 12 muffins.

Grandma's Biscuits

2 cups all-purpose flour
1 tablespoon baking powder
1 teaspoon salt
5 tablespoons vegetable shortening, butter or margarine
3/4 cup milk

To serve:
Butter or margarine

1. Preheat oven to 450F (230C).
2. Sift flour, baking powder and salt into a large bowl. With a pastry blender or 2 knives, cut in shortening, butter or margarine until mixture resembles coarse crumbs. Stir milk into flour mixture with a fork to make a soft dough.
3. On a lightly floured surface, knead dough 10 strokes. Roll out dough to 1/2 inch thick. Cut dough with a floured 2- to 2-1/2-inch-round cutter.
4. Place biscuits on an ungreased baking sheet about 1 inch apart for crusty biscuits or close together for soft biscuits.
5. Bake in preheated oven 12 to 15 minutes or until golden brown. Remove from baking sheet; serve hot with butter or margarine. Makes 12 biscuits.

Silver-Dollar Pancakes

1-1/2 cups sifted all-purpose flour
2 tablespoons sugar
2 teaspoons baking powder
1/2 teaspoon salt
1 egg, beaten
1/4 cup vegetable oil
1-1/4 cups milk

To serve:
Butter, margarine, preserves or jam

1. In a large bowl, combine flour, sugar, baking powder and salt. In a small bowl, beat egg, oil and milk until blended. Stir egg mixture into flour mixture until dry ingredients are barely moistened.
2. Heat a griddle or large skillet over medium heat. Brush hot griddle or skillet with vegetable oil.
3. Drop batter by tablespoons onto hot oiled griddle or skillet, a few at a time. Cook over medium heat until bubbles appear on top of pancake and edges are browned. Turn pancakes with a wide spatula; cook until bottom is golden. Remove cooked pancakes; keep warm. Repeat with remaining batter.
4. Serve warm pancakes with butter, margarine, preserves or jam. Makes 18 to 24 small pancakes.

Left to right: Silver-Dollar Pancakes; Walnut Brownies, page 42; Raisin-Bran Muffins

Cinnamon-Apple Muffins

2 cups all-purpose flour
1/3 cup firmly packed light-brown sugar
1 tablespoon baking powder
1 teaspoon salt
1 teaspoon ground cinnamon
1/2 teaspoon freshly grated nutmeg
3/4 cup milk
2 eggs
3 tablespoons vegetable oil
1 tablespoon lemon juice
1 cup finely chopped, peeled, tart apple (1 large apple)

---

1. Preheat oven to 400F (205C). Grease a 12-cup muffin pan or line cups with paper cupcake liners.
2. In a large bowl, combine flour, brown sugar, baking powder, salt, cinnamon and nutmeg.
3. In a small bowl, beat milk, eggs, oil and lemon juice until blended. Make a well in center of dry ingredients; stir in milk mixture until dry ingredients are barely moistened. Fold in chopped apple. Spoon batter into prepared muffin cups, filling cups about two-thirds full.
4. Bake in preheated oven 20 to 25 minutes or until a wooden pick inserted in center of a muffin comes out clean. Remove from pan. Serve warm or cool completely on a wire rack. Makes 12 muffins.

Raisin-Bran Muffins

1/4 cup vegetable oil
1/2 cup firmly packed light-brown sugar
1 egg
1 cup milk
1 cup all-purpose flour
1 cup unprocessed bran
1 tablespoon baking powder
1/2 teaspoon baking soda
1/2 teaspoon salt
1/2 cup raisins

---

1. Preheat oven to 400F (205C). Grease a 12-cup muffin pan or line muffin cups with paper cupcake liners.
2. In a medium bowl, beat oil, brown sugar, egg and milk until blended. In another medium bowl, combine flour, bran, baking powder, baking soda and salt. Stir flour mixture into milk mixture until combined. Fold in raisins.
3. Spoon batter into prepared muffin cups, filling cups about two-thirds full.
4. Bake in preheated oven 18 to 22 minutes or until a wooden pick inserted in center of a muffin comes out clean. Remove from pan. Serve warm or cool completely on a wire rack. Makes 12 muffins.

Cool-Rise White Bread

2 (1/4-oz.) pkgs. active dry yeast (2 tablespoons)
1/3 cup plus 1 teaspoon sugar
1-1/2 cups warm water (110F, 45C)
1/2 cup butter or margarine
2 teaspoons salt
1/2 cup milk, scalded
About 6-1/2 cups all-purpose flour or bread flour
1 egg beaten with 1 tablespoon milk for glaze

1. In a large bowl, dissolve yeast and 1 teaspoon sugar in warm water. Let stand 5 to 10 minutes or until foamy.
2. Stir remaining sugar, butter or margarine and salt into hot milk until butter or margarine melts. Cool to room temperature.
3. Stir cooled milk mixture into yeast mixture until blended. Add 5 cups flour; stir until combined. Stir in enough remaining flour to make a soft dough that comes away from side of bowl.
4. On a lightly floured surface, knead in enough remaining flour to make a stiff dough. Knead 8 to 10 minutes or until smooth and elastic.
5. Cover dough with plastic wrap and a dry towel. Let rest 20 minutes.
6. Grease 2 (9" x 5") loaf pans. Divide dough in half. Shape each piece into a loaf; place in greased pans. Brush tops lightly with vegetable oil.
7. Cover loaves loosely with plastic wrap. Refrigerate at least 2 hours or overnight.
8. Preheat oven to 375F (190C). Let loaves stand at room temperature 20 minutes before baking. Brush tops of loaves with egg glaze.
9. Bake in preheated oven 35 to 40 minutes or until bread sounds hollow when tapped on bottom. Remove from pans; cool completely on a wire rack. Makes 2 loaves.

Harvest-Time Bread

1/3 recipe White Bread, page 66
1 egg beaten with 1 tablespoon milk for glaze
2 currants

1. Prepare dough as directed through step 6, page 66. Grease a baking sheet. Cut dough into 3 equal pieces.
2. To make basic wheat sheaf, on a lightly floured surface, roll out 1 piece of dough about 12 inches long, 10 inches across top, making top rounded, and 8 inches across bottom. Place on greased baking sheet. Brush dough all over with egg glaze.
3. Cut second piece of dough into 4 equal pieces. Cut each piece into 6 pieces, making 24 small pieces.
4. Roll small pieces into 5-inch strips. Set 3 strips aside. Vertically place remaining 21 strips next to each other on bottom 1/3 of wheat sheaf to form stalks. Brush strips with egg glaze. Twist 2 reserved strips together to form tie; place horizontally across wheat sheaf along top edge of stalks. Brush with egg glaze. Shape remaining strip into a small oval field mouse; place in stalks. Use currants for eyes.
5. Roll out remaining piece of dough to a 16" x 8" rectangle. Cut dough lengthwise into 8 (1-inch-wide) strips. Cut strips on sharp diagonals, making small diamond-shaped pieces.
6. Attach a row of diamonds to outside edge of sheaf, starting at bottom left above tie. Fill in with remaining diamonds, working from top to bottom. Overlap diamonds, brushing with glaze as you go. Fill in top 2/3 of wheat sheaf completely with diamonds to make wheat heads.
7. Cover with a dry towel; let rise in a warm place, free from drafts, 15 to 20 minutes.
8. Preheat oven to 375F (190C). Brush sheaf all over with egg glaze.
9. Bake in preheated oven 30 to 35 minutes or until deep golden brown. Cool on baking sheet on a wire rack 10 minutes. Carefully slide sheaf from baking sheet to wire rack; cool completely on rack. Makes 1 wheat sheaf.

Harvest-Time Bread

White Bread

3 (1/4-oz.) pkgs. active dry yeast (3 tablespoons)
1/4 cup plus 2 teaspoons sugar
1-1/2 cups warm water (110F, 45C)
1/3 cup butter or margarine
4 teaspoons salt
2 cups milk, scalded
8-1/2 to 9 cups all-purpose flour or bread flour
1 egg yolk beaten with 1 tablespoon milk for glaze

1. In a large bowl, dissolve yeast and 2 teaspoons sugar in warm water. Let stand 5 to 10 minutes or until foamy.
2. Add remaining sugar, butter or margarine and salt to hot milk; stir until butter or margarine melts. Cool to room temperature.
3. Stir cooled milk mixture into yeast mixture until blended. Stir in 6 cups flour until combined. Stir in enough remaining flour to make a soft dough that comes away from side of bowl.
4. On a lightly floured surface, knead in enough remaining flour to make a stiff dough. Knead 8 to 10 minutes or until smooth and elastic.
5. Clean and grease bowl. Place dough in greased bowl, turning to coat all sides. Cover with a slightly damp towel. Let rise in a warm place, free from drafts, until doubled in bulk, 1 to 1-1/2 hours.
6. Grease 3 (9" x 5") loaf pans. Punch down dough; divide dough into 3 equal pieces. Shape each piece into a loaf, pinching and tucking ends under. Place loaves in greased pans. Cover with a dry towel; let rise until doubled in bulk.
7. Preheat oven to 375F (190C). Brush tops of loaves with egg-yolk glaze.
8. Bake in preheated oven 35 to 40 minutes or until bread sounds hollow when tapped on bottom. Remove from pans; cool on wire racks. Makes 3 loaves.

Variations

Buttered Split Loaves: Prepare dough; let rise as directed above. Punch down dough; divide into 3 equal pieces. Shape loaves; place in greased 9" x 5" loaf pans. Cover and let rise until doubled in bulk. Split top of each loaf lengthwise with a sharp razor blade. Pour 2 tablespoons melted butter or margarine into each split. Brush remainder of loaf top with egg-yolk glaze; bake.
Free-Form Loaves: Prepare dough; let rise as directed above. Grease baking sheets. Punch down dough; divide into 3 equal pieces. Shape each piece into an 11-inch round or oval loaf. Place loaves on greased baking sheets. Cut several diagonal slashes on top of each loaf with a sharp razor blade or sharp knife. Cover and let rise until doubled. Brush with egg-yolk glaze; bake according to directions above.

1/To knead, bring dough toward you.

2/Push dough down and away from you.

3/Punch down dough to remove air.

4/Cut several diagonal slashes on top of loaf.

Poppy-Seed Braid

1 (1/4-oz.) pkg. active dry yeast (1 tablespoon)
1 tablespoon plus 1 teaspoon sugar
1-1/4 cups warm water (110F, 45C)
1-1/2 teaspoons salt
2 tablespoons butter or margarine, melted, cooled
About 3-1/4 cups all-purpose flour or bread flour
1 egg yolk beaten with 1 tablespoon milk for glaze
Poppy seeds

1. In a large bowl, dissolve yeast and 1 teaspoon sugar in warm water. Let stand 5 to 10 minutes or until foamy.
2. Add remaining sugar, salt and butter or margarine to yeast mixture; stir until blended. Stir in 2-1/2 cups flour until combined. Stir in enough remaining flour to make a soft dough that comes away from side of bowl.
3. On a lightly floured surface, knead in enough remaining flour to make a stiff dough. Continue kneading 8 to 10 minutes or until smooth and elastic.
4. Clean and grease bowl. Place dough in greased bowl, turning to coat all sides. Cover with a slightly damp towel. Let rise in a warm place, free from drafts, until doubled in bulk, about 1 hour.
5. Grease a baking sheet. Punch down dough; divide into 3 equal pieces. Shape each piece into a 18-inch-long rope. Braid ropes together to form a loaf, pinching and tucking ends under. Place loaf on greased baking sheet. Cover with a dry towel; let rise until almost doubled in bulk.
6. Preheat oven to 375F (190C). Brush bread with egg-yolk glaze; sprinkle with poppy seeds.
7. Bake in preheated oven 35 to 40 minutes or until bread sounds hollow when tapped on bottom. Remove from baking sheet; cool on a wire rack. Makes 1 loaf.

Whole-Wheat Bread

1 (1/4-oz.) pkg. active dry yeast (1 tablespoon)
1 teaspoon granulated sugar
1-1/4 cups warm water (110F, 45C)
1/4 cup firmly packed dark-brown sugar
2 tablespoons butter or margarine, melted, cooled
1-1/2 teaspoons salt
2 cups whole-wheat flour
About 1-1/4 cups all-purpose flour or bread flour
Milk or water
Cracked wheat or oat flakes

---

1. In a large bowl, dissolve yeast and 1 teaspoon granulated sugar in warm water. Let stand 5 to 10 minutes or until foamy.
2. Stir brown sugar, butter or margarine and salt into yeast mixture until blended. Stir in whole-wheat flour and 3/4 cup all-purpose flour or bread flour until blended. Stir in enough remaining all-purpose flour or bread flour to make a soft dough that comes away from side of bowl.
3. On a lightly floured surface, knead in enough remaining all-purpose flour or bread flour to make a stiff dough. Knead 8 to 10 minutes or until smooth and elastic.
4. Clean and grease bowl. Place dough in greased bowl, turning to coat all sides. Cover with a slightly damp towel. Let rise in a warm place, free from drafts, until doubled in bulk, about 1 hour.
5. Grease a baking sheet. Punch down dough; shape into a round loaf, pinching and tucking side under. Cut a deep cross on top of loaf with a sharp razor blade. Cover with a dry towel; let rise until almost doubled in bulk.
6. Preheat oven to 400F (205C). Brush top of bread with milk or water; sprinkle with cracked wheat or oat flakes. Bake in preheated oven 30 to 35 minutes or until bread sounds hollow when tapped on bottom. Remove from baking sheet; cool on a wire rack. Makes 1 loaf.

Variations
Traditional Loaf: Prepare dough; let rise as directed above. Grease a 9" x 5" loaf pan. Punch down dough; shape into a loaf, pinching and tucking ends under. Place in greased pan. Cover and let rise until doubled. Bake as directed above.
Rolls: Prepare dough; let rise as directed above. Grease a 12-cup muffin pan or a 13" x 9" baking pan. Punch down dough; shape into 12 equal balls, pinching and tucking sides under. Place balls, seam-side down, in greased muffin cups, or arrange balls in greased baking pan, allowing room for expansion. Cover and let dough in muffin cups rise 20 to 30 minutes; let rolls in pan rise 50 to 60 minutes. Bake in preheated 400F (205C) oven 15 to 20 minutes or until rolls sound hollow when tapped on bottom.

Top to bottom: Poppy-Seed Braid, Free-Form White Bread, Whole-Wheat Bread

Vienna Rolls

1 (1/4-oz.) pkg. active dry yeast (1 tablespoon)
3 tablespoons plus 1 teaspoon sugar
1/2 cup warm water (110F, 45C)
1/4 cup butter or margarine
1-1/2 teaspoons salt
3/4 cup milk, scalded
About 3-1/4 cups all-purpose flour or bread flour
1 egg yolk beaten with 1 tablespoon milk for glaze
Poppy seeds, if desired

---

1. In a large bowl, dissolve yeast and 1 teaspoon sugar in warm water. Let stand 5 to 10 minutes or until foamy.
2. Stir remaining sugar, butter or margarine and salt into hot milk until butter or margarine melts. Cool to room temperature.
3. Stir cooled milk mixture into yeast mixture until blended. Stir in 2-1/2 cups flour until combined. Stir in enough remaining flour to make a soft dough that comes away from side of bowl.
4. On a lightly floured surface, knead in enough remaining flour to make a stiff dough. Knead 8 to 10 minutes or until smooth and elastic.
5. Clean and grease bowl. Place dough in greased bowl, turning to coat all sides. Cover with a slightly damp towel. Let rise in a warm place, free from drafts, until doubled in bulk, about 1 hour.
6. Lightly grease baking sheets. Punch down dough; cut dough into 16 equal pieces. Shape each piece into desired shape; see below. Place shaped rolls 2 to 3 inches apart on greased baking sheets. Cover with a dry towel; let rise until almost doubled in bulk.
7. Preheat oven to 400F (205C). Brush rolls with egg-yolk glaze; sprinkle with poppy seeds, if desired.
8. Bake in preheated oven 18 to 20 minutes or until golden brown. Remove from baking sheets; cool on wire racks. Serve warm. Makes 16 rolls.

Cloverleaf: Cut each piece of dough into 3 small pieces. Shape each piece into a ball, pinching and tucking sides under. Place balls in sets of 3, barely touching each other, on greased baking sheets.
Knots: Shape each piece of dough into an 8-inch-long rope. Tie in a knot.
Figure 8: Shape each piece of dough into an 8-inch-long rope. Curl opposite ends toward center to make a figure 8.
Ovals: Shape each piece of dough into a small oval loaf. Cut 2 or 3 diagonal slashes on top of roll with a sharp razor blade.
Braid: Divide each piece of dough into 3 equal pieces. Shape each piece into an 8-inch-long rope. Braid ropes; tuck ends under.
Snails: Shape each piece of dough into an 8-inch-long rope. Coil rope into a snail shape.
Cottage: Divide each piece of dough into 2 pieces, making 1 piece slightly larger than the other. Shape both pieces into balls, pinching and tucking sides under. Place large ball on greased baking sheet; top with small ball. Using the handle of a small wooden spoon, poke hole in center of small ball down through large ball to baking sheet.

Vienna Rolls

Currant Bread

1 (1/4-oz.) pkg. active dry yeast (1 tablespoon)
3 tablespoons plus 1 teaspoon sugar
1/4 cup warm water (110F, 45C)
2 tablespoons butter or margarine
1 teaspoon salt
1 cup milk, scalded
About 3-1/4 cups all-purpose flour or bread flour
1 cup currants
Honey

1. In a large bowl, dissolve yeast and 1 teaspoon sugar in warm water. Let stand 5 to 10 minutes or until foamy.
2. Stir remaining sugar, butter or margarine and salt into hot milk until butter or margarine melts. Cool to room temperature.
3. Stir cooled milk mixture into yeast mixture until blended. Stir in 2 cups flour and currants until combined. Stir in enough remaining flour to make a soft dough that comes away from side of bowl.
4. On a lightly floured surface, knead in enough remaining flour to make a stiff dough. Knead 8 to 10 minutes or until smooth and elastic.
5. Clean and grease bowl. Place dough in greased bowl, turning to coat all sides. Cover with a slightly damp towel. Let rise in a warm place, free from drafts, until doubled in bulk, about 1 hour.
6. Grease a 9" x 5" loaf pan. Punch down dough. Shape dough into a loaf, pinching and tucking ends under. Place in greased pan. Cover with a dry towel; let rise until doubled in bulk.
7. Preheat oven to 375F (190C). Brush top of bread with water.
8. Bake in preheated oven 35 to 40 minutes or until bread sounds hollow when tapped on bottom. Remove bread from pan; brush top with honey while still warm. Cool on a wire rack. Makes 1 loaf.

Whole-Wheat & Rye Twists

2 (1/4-oz.) pkgs. active dry yeast (2 tablespoons)
1/4 cup plus 1 teaspoon firmly packed
   dark-brown sugar
2 cups warm water (110F, 45C)
1/4 cup butter or margarine, melted, cooled
1 tablespoon salt
4 cups whole-wheat flour
2 cups medium rye flour
1 egg white beaten with 1 tablespoon water for glaze

1. In a large bowl, dissolve yeast and 1 teaspoon brown sugar in warm water. Let stand 5 to 10 minutes or until foamy.
2. Stir remaining brown sugar, butter or margarine and salt into yeast mixture until blended. Stir whole-wheat flour and rye flour together until blended. Add 4-1/2 cups of flour mixture; stir until combined. Stir in enough remaining flour mixture to make a soft dough that comes away from side of bowl.
3. On a lightly floured surface, knead in enough remaining flour mixture to make a stiff dough. Knead 8 to 10 minutes or until smooth and elastic.
4. Clean and grease bowl. Place dough in greased bowl, turning to coat all sides. Cover with a slightly damp towel. Let rise in a warm place, free from drafts, until doubled in bulk, about 1-1/4 hours.
5. Grease 2 baking sheets. Punch down dough; cut into 2 equal pieces. Cut each piece in half. Shape pieces into 16-inch-long ropes. Twist 2 ropes together; tuck ends under. Repeat with remaining 2 ropes. Place loaves on greased baking sheets. Cover with a dry towel; let rise until doubled in bulk.
6. Preheat oven to 400F (205C). Brush loaves with egg-white glaze.
7. Bake in preheated oven 35 to 40 minutes or until bread sounds hollow when tapped on bottom. Remove from baking sheets; cool completely on a wire rack. Makes 2 loaves.

Left to right: Currant Bread, Whole-Wheat & Rye Twist, Cheese & Herb Bread, Buttermilk Cottage Loaf

Cheese & Herb Bread

2 tablespoons butter or margarine
1 small onion, finely chopped
1 (1/4-oz.) pkg. active dry yeast (1 tablespoon)
2 tablespoons plus 1 teaspoon sugar
1-1/4 cups warm water (110F, 45C)
1-1/2 teaspoons salt
1 teaspoon dry mustard
1 tablespoon chopped mixed fresh herbs or
   1 teaspoon Italian seasoning
2 cups whole-wheat flour
1-1/4 cups shredded sharp Cheddar cheese (6 oz.)
About 1-1/4 cups all-purpose flour or bread flour

---

1. Melt butter or margarine in a small skillet over medium heat. Add onion; sauté until golden. Let cool.
2. In a large bowl, dissolve yeast and 1 teaspoon sugar in warm water. Let stand 5 to 10 minutes or until foamy.
3. Stir remaining sugar, salt, mustard, herbs or Italian seasoning and cooled onion into yeast mixture until combined. Stir in whole-wheat flour and 1 cup Cheddar cheese until combined. Stir in enough all-purpose flour or bread flour to make a soft dough that comes away from side of bowl.
4. On a lightly floured surface, knead in enough remaining all-purpose flour or bread flour to make a stiff dough. Knead 8 to 10 minutes or until smooth and elastic.
5. Clean and grease bowl. Place dough in greased bowl, turning to coat all sides. Cover with a slightly damp towel. Let rise in a warm place, free from drafts, until doubled in bulk, about 1 hour.
6. Grease a 9" x 5" loaf pan. Punch down dough; shape into a loaf, pinching and tucking ends under. Place in greased pan. Cover with a dry towel; let rise until doubled in bulk.
7. Preheat oven to 375F (190C). Brush top of bread with water; sprinkle with remaining 1/4 cup Cheddar cheese.
8. Bake in preheated oven 35 to 40 minutes or until bread sounds hollow when tapped on bottom. Remove from pan; cool completely on a wire rack. Makes 1 loaf.

Buttermilk Cottage Loaf

1 cup buttermilk
1/3 cup butter or margarine, room temperature
1 (1/4-oz.) pkg. active dry yeast (1 tablespoon)
1/4 cup plus 1 teaspoon sugar
3/4 cup warm water (110F, 45C)
2 teaspoons salt
1/2 teaspoon baking soda
About 5 cups all-purpose flour or bread flour
1 egg yolk beaten with 1 tablespoon milk for glaze

---

1. In a small saucepan over low heat, heat buttermilk and butter or margarine, stirring, until butter or margarine melts. Cool to room temperature.
2. In a large bowl, dissolve yeast and 1 teaspoon sugar in warm water. Let stand 5 to 10 minutes or until foamy.
3. Stir cooled buttermilk mixture, remaining sugar and salt into yeast mixture until blended. Add baking soda and 3-1/2 cups flour; stir until combined. Stir in enough remaining flour to make a soft dough that comes away from side of bowl.
4. On a lightly floured surface, knead in enough remaining flour to make a stiff dough. Knead 8 to 10 minutes or until smooth and elastic.
5. Clean and grease bowl. Place dough in greased bowl, turning to coat all sides. Cover with a slightly damp towel. Let rise in a warm place, free from drafts, until doubled in bulk, 1 to 1-1/2 hours.
6. Grease a baking sheet. Punch down dough; divide into 2 pieces, making 1 piece 2/3 of dough. Shape large piece of dough into a slightly flattened ball; place on greased baking sheet. Shape small piece of dough into a ball; place on top of large piece of dough. Flour a wooden spoon handle; poke through center of small ball down through large ball to baking sheet. Cover with a dry towel; let rise until doubled in bulk. Brush with egg-yolk glaze.
7. Preheat oven to 400F (205C).
8. Bake in preheated oven 40 to 45 minutes or until bread sounds hollow when tapped on bottom. Remove from baking sheet and cool completely on a wire rack. Makes 1 large loaf.

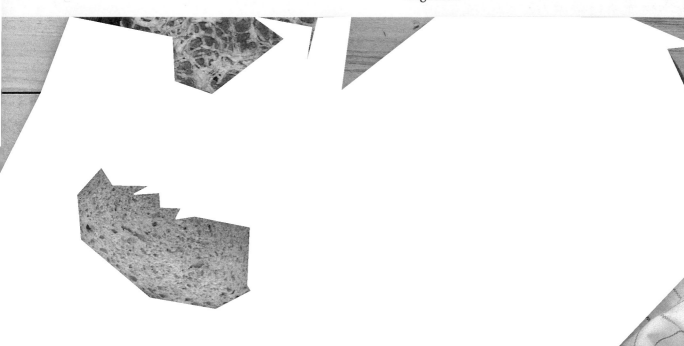

Rum Savarin

1 (1/4-oz.) pkg. active dry yeast (1 tablespoon)
2 tablespoons plus 1 teaspoon sugar
1/3 cup warm milk (110F, 45C)
2 cups sifted all-purpose flour
1/2 teaspoon salt
3 eggs, beaten
1/3 cup butter or margarine, melted, cooled

Rum Syrup:
1/2 cup sugar
1 cup water
1/3 to 1/2 cup dark rum

To serve:
2 cups sweetened whipped cream
Sliced strawberries, bananas, raspberries or peaches

1. Grease an 8- or 9-inch ring mold or savarin mold. In a medium bowl, dissolve yeast and 1 teaspoon sugar in warm milk. Let stand 5 to 10 minutes or until foamy.
2. Stir remaining sugar, 1 cup flour and salt into yeast mixture until combined. Add remaining flour, eggs and butter or margarine; beat vigorously with a wooden spoon 2 to 3 minutes or until batter is smooth.
3. Spoon batter into greased mold, spreading evenly.
4. Cover with a slightly damp towel. Let rise in a warm place, free from drafts, until dough almost reaches rim of pan, about 1 hour.
5. Preheat oven to 375F (190C).
6. Bake in preheated oven 25 to 30 minutes or until top is golden brown. Remove from pan; cool on a wire rack.
7. To make syrup, combine sugar and water in a medium saucepan over medium heat; stir until sugar is dissolved. Boil 5 minutes or until syrupy, without stirring. Cool slightly. Stir in rum.
8. Place cooled savarin in a deep serving dish; prick all over with a fork. Slowly pour warm syrup over savarin; let stand until syrup has been absorbed.
9. To serve, spoon whipped cream into center; fill with fruit. Makes 8 to 10 servings.

Apple-Filled Doughnuts

Apple-Filled Doughnuts

1 (1/4-oz.) pkg. active dry yeast (1 tablespoon)
3 tablespoons plus 1 teaspoon sugar
3/4 cup warm milk (110F, 45C)
1/4 cup butter or margarine, melted, cooled
1 egg, beaten
1 teaspoon salt
About 3 cups all-purpose flour flour
1 cup chunk-style applesauce
Vegetable oil for deep-frying
2 teaspoons ground cinnamon mixed with 1/3 cup sugar

1. In a large bowl, dissolve yeast and 1 teaspoon sugar in warm milk. Let stand 5 to 10 minutes or until foamy.
2. Stir remaining sugar, butter or margarine, egg and salt into yeast mixture until blended. Add 2-1/4 cups flour; stir until combined. Stir in enough remaining flour to make a soft dough that comes away from side of bowl.
3. On a lightly floured surface, knead in enough flour to make a stiff dough. Knead 8 to 10 minutes or until smooth and elastic.
4. Clean and grease bowl. Place dough in greased bowl, turning to coat all sides. Cover with a slightly damp towel. Let rise in a warm place, free from drafts, until doubled in bulk, about 1 hour.
5. Grease 2 baking sheets. Punch down dough; cut into 24 equal pieces. On a lightly floured surface, roll out each piece of dough to a 4-inch circle. Place 1 teaspoon applesauce in center of each circle. Brush edges of dough lightly with water. Gather edges; draw up to enclose filling completely. Pinch to seal. Place filled balls, seam-side down, on greased baking sheets about 2 inches apart. Cover with a dry towel; let rise 30 minutes.
6. Heat oil in a deep-fat fryer to 350F (175C) or until a 1-inch bread cube turns golden brown in 50 seconds. Carefully drop doughnuts, a few at a time, into hot oil. Deep-fry until doughnuts are puffed and golden brown. Remove with a slotted spoon; drain on paper towels. Repeat with remaining doughnuts.
7. Place cinnamon-sugar mixture in a medium bowl. Add warm doughnuts, a few at a time; toss to coat with sugar mixture. Makes 24 doughnuts.

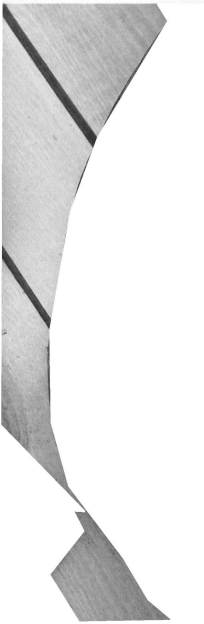

Sesame-Seed Breadsticks

2 (1/4-oz.) pkgs. active dry yeast (2 tablespoons)
1 tablespoon sugar
1-1/2 cups warm water (110F, 45C)
1/4 cup vegetable oil
2 teaspoons salt
About 3-1/2 cups all-purpose flour or bread flour
1 egg white beaten with 1 tablespoon water for glaze
About 1/2 cup raw sesame seeds

1. In a large bowl, dissolve yeast and 1 teaspoon sugar in warm water. Let stand 5 to 10 minutes or until foamy.
2. Stir remaining sugar, oil, salt and 1/2 cup flour into yeast mixture until well blended. Add about 2-1/2 cups flour; beat vigorously with a wooden spoon until dough is soft and shiny and comes away from side of bowl.
3. On a lightly floured surface, knead in enough remaining flour to make a stiff dough. Knead 8 to 10 minutes or until smooth and elastic.
4. Cover dough with a dry towel; let rest 15 minutes.
5. Preheat oven to 350F (175C). Grease 2 baking sheets. Shape dough into a 24-inch-long rope; cut into 24 (1-inch) pieces. Roll each piece into a 12-inch stick.
6. Brush breadsticks with egg-white glaze; sprinkle with sesame seeds. Place breadsticks about 1-1/2 inches apart on greased baking sheets.
7. Bake in preheated oven 30 to 35 minutes or until golden brown. Remove from baking sheets; cool on wire racks. Serve warm or let cool completely. Makes 24 breadsticks.

Parkerhouse Rolls

1 (1/4-oz.) pkg. active dry yeast (1 tablespoon)
3 tablespoons plus 1 teaspoon sugar
1/2 cup warm water (110F, 45C)
1/4 cup butter or margarine
1 teaspoon salt
1/2 cup milk, scalded
1 egg
About 3-1/4 cups all-purpose flour
About 1/4 cup butter or margarine, melted

1. In a large bowl, dissolve yeast and 1 teaspoon sugar in warm water. Let stand 5 to 10 minutes or until foamy.
2. Stir remaining sugar, 1/4 cup butter or margarine and salt into hot milk until butter or margarine melts. Cool to room temperature.
3. Stir cooled milk mixture and egg into yeast mixture until blended. Add 2-1/2 cups flour; stir until combined. Stir in enough remaining flour to make a soft dough that comes away from side of bowl.
4. On a lightly floured surface, knead in enough remaining flour to make a stiff dough. Knead 8 to 10 minutes or until smooth and elastic.
5. Clean and grease bowl. Place dough in greased bowl, turning to coat all sides. Cover with a slightly damp towel. Let rise in a warm place, free from drafts, until doubled in bulk, about 1 hour.
6. Grease a 15" x 10" jelly-roll pan. Punch down dough. Divide dough in half; roll out 1 piece of dough to about 1/2 inch thick. Cut with a floured 2-1/2- to 3-inch plain cookie cutter. Repeat with remaining piece of dough. Gather dough scraps; reroll. Cut as many circles as possible.
7. Brush circles with melted butter or margarine. Press handle of a wooden spoon across each circle, slightly off center, to make a crease. Fold circles almost in half along crease with smaller portion on top; press edges lightly together. Place rolls fairly close together in greased pan. Cover with a dry towel; let rise until almost doubled in bulk.
8. Preheat oven to 400F (205C). Brush rolls with melted butter or margarine.
9. Bake in preheated oven 15 to 20 minutes or until rolls are golden brown. Remove from baking sheets; serve warm. Makes 16 to 20 rolls.

Almond-Filled Loaf

1 (1/4-oz.) pkg. active dry yeast (1 tablespoon)
1/4 cup plus 1 teaspoon sugar
1/2 cup warm milk (110F, 45C)
1/4 cup butter or margarine, melted, cooled
1/2 teaspoon salt
1 egg, beaten
About 2-1/3 cups all-purpose flour
1 egg yolk beaten with 1 tablespoon milk for glaze

Filling:
3/4 cup finely ground blanched almonds
1/3 cup sugar
1 egg white, beaten
1 tablespoon milk
1/2 teaspoon almond extract
1/4 cup chopped red candied cherries
2 tablespoons raisins

Icing:
1 cup powdered sugar, sifted
1 to 2 tablespoons hot water

To decorate:
1 to 2 tablespoons toasted sliced or slivered almonds
Red candied cherries, quartered

1. In a large bowl, dissolve yeast and 1 teaspoon sugar in warm milk. Let stand 5 to 10 minutes or until foamy.
2. Stir remaining sugar, butter or margarine, salt and egg into yeast mixture until blended. Stir in 1-3/4 cups flour until combined. Stir in enough remaining flour to make a soft dough that comes away from side of bowl.
3. On a lightly floured surface, knead in enough remaining flour to make a stiff dough. Knead 8 to 10 minutes or until smooth and elastic.
4. Clean and grease bowl. Place dough in greased bowl, turning to coat all sides. Cover with a slightly damp towel. Let rise in a warm place, free from drafts, until doubled in bulk, about 1 hour.
5. To make filling, in a small bowl, blend ground almonds and sugar. Stir in egg white, milk and almond extract until thoroughly blended. Set aside.
6. Grease a 9" x 5" loaf pan. Punch down dough. On a lightly floured surface, roll out dough to a 12" x 9" rectangle. Spread almond mixture over dough to within 1/4 inch of edges. Sprinkle chopped cherries and raisins over almond mixture. Roll, jelly-roll style, starting at 1 short end. Pinch ends to seal. Place filled loaf, seam-side down, in greased pan. Cover with a dry towel; let rise until doubled in bulk.
7. Preheat oven to 375F (190C). Brush top of loaf with egg-yolk glaze.
8. Bake in preheated oven 35 to 40 minutes or until top is deep golden brown and loaf sounds hollow when tapped on bottom. Remove from pan; cool on a wire rack.
9. To make icing, in a small bowl, stir powdered sugar and 1 tablespoon water until smooth, adding more water if necessary. Spoon icing on top of loaf; decorate loaf with toasted almonds and cherries quarters. Let stand until icing is set. Makes 1 loaf.

Fruity Raisin Buns

2 teaspoons active dry yeast
2 tablespoons plus 1 teaspoon granulated sugar
1/2 cup warm milk (110F, 45C)
1 egg, beaten
2 tablespoons butter or margarine, room temperature
1/2 teaspoon salt
1-1/2 cups all-purpose flour
1/2 cup raisins
2 tablespoons chopped candied orange peel or
   lemon peel
1 egg yolk beaten with 1 tablespoon milk for glaze
Crystal sugar or crushed sugar cubes

1. In a large bowl, dissolve yeast and 1 teaspoon granulated sugar in warm milk. Let stand 5 to 10 minutes or until foamy.
2. Stir remaining granulated sugar, egg, butter or margarine and salt into yeast mixture; stir until blended. Add flour; beat with a wooden spoon 2 minutes. Stir in raisins and candied peel until combined.
3. Cover with a slightly damp towel. Let rise in a warm place, free from drafts, until doubled in bulk, about 1 hour.
4. Grease 2 baking sheets. Stir down dough with a wooden spoon. Drop by heaping tablespoons 2 to 3 inches apart on greased baking sheets. Brush buns with egg-yolk glaze; sprinkle with coarse sugar. Cover loosely with a dry towel; let rise until almost doubled in bulk.
5. Preheat oven to 400F (205C).
6. Bake buns in preheated oven 12 to 15 minutes or until golden brown. Remove from baking sheets; cool on wire racks. Serve warm with butter or margarine. Makes 14 buns.

Left to right: Fruity Raisin Buns, Almond-Filled Loaf

Danish Pastries

1 (1/4-oz.) pkg. active dry yeast (1 tablespoon)
2 tablespoons plus 1 teaspoon sugar
1/4 cup warm water (110F, 45C)
3/4 cup butter or margarine
1/2 teaspoon salt
1/2 cup milk, scalded
1 egg
1 egg yolk
1/2 teaspoon ground mace
About 2-1/2 cups all-purpose flour
2 tablespoons all-purpose flour

Spice Filling:
1/4 cup butter or margarine, room temperature
2 tablespoons sugar
1 teaspoon ground cinnamon
1/4 cup currants

Almond Filling:
1/3 cup finely ground almonds
2 tablespoons sugar
1 tablespoon egg white
1 egg yolk beaten with 1 tablespoon milk for glaze

Icing:
1 cup powdered sugar, sifted
1-1/2 tablespoons warm water

---

1. In a medium bowl, dissolve yeast and 1 teaspoon sugar in warm water. Let stand 5 to 10 minutes or until foamy.
2. Stir remaining sugar, 1/4 cup butter or margarine and salt into hot milk until butter or margarine melts. Cool to room temperature. Stir cooled milk mixture, egg and egg yolk into yeast mixture until combined.
3. Add mace and 1-3/4 cups flour; stir until combined. Stir in enough remaining flour to make a soft dough that comes away from side of bowl.
4. On a lightly floured surface, knead in enough remaining flour to make a stiff dough. Knead 8 to 10 minutes or until smooth and elastic.
5. Cover dough with a dry towel; let rest 30 minutes.
6. In a small bowl, blend remaining 1/2 cup butter or margarine with 2 tablespoons flour; shape into a 5" x 4" rectangle. Refrigerate until almost firm.
7. On a lightly floured surface, roll out dough to a 15" x 5" rectangle. Place chilled block of butter or margarine lengthwise in center of dough. Fold 1/3 of dough over butter or margarine. Fold remaining dough over dough-covered butter or margarine. Press edges to seal.
8. Roll out dough to a 15" x 5" rectangle; fold in thirds. Wrap in plastic wrap or waxed paper; refrigerate 20 minutes.
9. Repeat rolling and folding dough 2 times, for a total of 3 times. Wrap and refrigerate dough 20 minutes after second rolling and folding. Wrap and refrigerate dough 30 minutes after last folding and rolling.

10. To make spice filling, in a small bowl, beat butter or margarine, sugar and cinnamon until smooth. Fold in currants.
11. To make almond filling, in a small bowl, stir almonds, sugar and egg white until blended.
12. Cut dough in half. Refrigerate 1/2 until needed. Roll out dough half to a 16" x 8" rectangle. Spread spice filling over dough; cut in half lengthwise. Roll 1 piece jelly-roll style, starting from short end. Cut into 4 equal slices. Place slices, cut-side down, on ungreased baking sheets. Brush with egg-yolk glaze. Fold remaining spice-filling-covered dough crosswise into thirds; cut into 4 equal strips from folded edge to folded edge. Twist ends of each strip in opposite directions; place on baking sheet. Brush with egg-yolk glaze.
13. Roll out reserved dough to a 16" x 8" rectangle. Cut into 8 (4-inch) squares. Shape almond filling into 8 flattened balls. Place 1 ball in center of each square. Cut squares diagonally from each corner in toward center almost to almond ball. Fold points in toward center to enclose filling; press down lightly to seal. Place on baking sheet. Brush with egg-yolk glaze. Cover pastries with a dry towel; let rise 30 to 40 minutes.
14. Preheat oven to 425F (220C). Brush pastries with egg-yolk glaze again.
15. Bake in preheated oven 10 to 12 minutes or until golden brown. Remove from baking sheets; cool on wire racks.
16. To make icing, in a small bowl, combine powdered sugar and water until smooth. Drizzle over pastries; let stand until set. Makes 16 pastries.

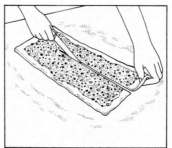

1/Spread spice filling over dough. Cut in half lengthwise.

2/Cut into 4 equal slices.

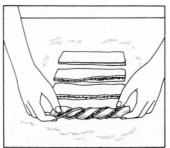

3/Twist ends of each strip in opposite directions.

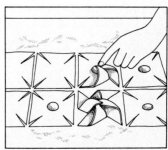

4/Fold points in toward center to enclose filling.

Cinnamon Rolls

1 (1/4-oz.) pkg. active dry yeast (1 tablespoon)
1/4 cup plus 1 teaspoon sugar
1 cup warm milk (110F, 45C)
1 teaspoon salt
6 tablespoons butter or margarine, melted, cooled
2 eggs, beaten
About 4 cups all-purpose flour
2 tablespoons butter or margarine, melted, cooled

Filling:
1/2 cup firmly packed light-brown sugar
2 teaspoons ground cinnamon
3/4 cup raisins or currants

Glaze:
2 cups sifted powdered sugar
1/2 teaspoon vanilla extract
3 tablespoons milk or water

1. In a large bowl, dissolve yeast and 1 teaspoon sugar in warm milk. Let stand 5 to 10 minutes or until foamy.
2. Stir remaining sugar, salt, 6 tablespoons butter or margarine and eggs into yeast mixture until blended. Add 3 cups flour; stir until combined. Stir in enough remaining flour to make a soft dough that comes away from side of bowl.
3. On a lightly floured surface, knead in enough remaining flour to make a stiff dough. Knead 8 to 10 minutes or until smooth and elastic.
4. Clean and grease bowl. Place dough in greased bowl, turning to coat all sides. Cover with a slightly damp towel. Let rise in a warm place, free from drafts, until doubled in bulk.
5. Grease a 13" x 9" baking pan. Punch down dough. On a lightly floured surface, roll out dough to an 18" x 12" rectangle. Brush with 2 tablespoons melted butter or margarine.
6. To make filling, in a small bowl, combine brown sugar, cinnamon and raisins or currants; sprinkle over dough.
7. Roll up dough, jelly-roll style, starting at 1 long end. Pinch seam to seal. Cut dough into 15 equal slices. Arrange slices, cut-side down, in greased pan, allowing room for expansion. Cover with a dry towel; let rise until almost doubled in bulk.
8. Preheat oven to 375F (190C).
9. Bake in preheated oven 25 to 30 minutes or until top is golden brown. Cool in pan on a wire rack.
10. To make glaze, in a small bowl, combine powdered sugar, vanilla and milk or water. Spread glaze over warm rolls in pan. Let stand until glaze is set. To serve, pull rolls apart with 2 forks; remove from pan. Makes 15 rolls.

Danish Pastries

Panettone

1/2 cup butter or margarine, room temperature
1/4 cup plus 1 teaspoon sugar
3 eggs
1 teaspoon salt
1 tablespoon grated lemon peel
1 (1/4-oz.) pkg. active dry yeast (1 tablespoon)
1/3 cup warm milk (110F, 45C)
About 3 cups all-purpose flour
3/4 cup raisins
1/2 cup chopped mixed candied fruit
1 egg yolk beaten with 1 tablespoon milk for glaze

---

1. In a large bowl, beat butter or margarine and 1/4 cup sugar 8 to 10 minutes or until light and fluffy. Beat in eggs, 1 at a time, beating well after each addition. Beat in salt and lemon peel until blended.
2. In a small bowl, dissolve yeast and remaining sugar in warm milk. Let stand 5 to 10 minutes or until foamy.
3. Stir egg mixture into yeast mixture until blended. Add 2 cups flour, raisins and mixed fruit; stir until combined. Stir in enough remaining flour to make a soft dough that comes away from side of bowl.
4. On a lightly floured surface, knead in enough remaining flour to make a stiff dough. Knead 8 to 10 minutes or until smooth and elastic.
5. Clean and grease bowl. Place dough in greased bowl, turning to coat all sides. Cover with a slightly damp towel. Let rise in a warm place, free from drafts, until doubled in bulk, about 1-1/2 hours.
6. Grease an 8-inch springform pan or deep cake pan. Punch down dough; shape into a round loaf, pinching and tucking sides under. Place shaped dough, seam-side down, in greased pan. Cover with a dry towel; let rise until doubled in bulk.
7. Preheat oven to 400F (205C). Brush loaf top with egg-yolk glaze.
8. Bake in preheated oven 10 minutes. Reduce oven temperature to 350F (175C); bake 30 to 35 minutes or until top is deep golden brown and loaf sounds hollow when tapped on bottom. Remove from pan; cool completely on a wire rack. Slice and serve with butter or margarine. Makes 1 loaf.

Hungarian Coffeecake

1 (1/4-oz.) pkg. active dry yeast (1 tablespoon)
3 tablespoons plus 1 teaspoon sugar
1/2 cup warm milk (110F, 45C)
1/4 cup butter or margarine, melted, cooled
1/2 teaspoon salt
1 egg, beaten
About 2-1/4 cups all-purpose flour
1 teaspoon ground cinnamon
1/4 cup sugar
1/4 cup finely chopped walnuts, pecans or almonds
1/4 cup raisins, chopped

Icing:
1 cup sifted powdered sugar
1 to 2 tablespoons milk

---

1. In a large bowl, dissolve yeast and 1 teaspoon sugar in warm milk. Let stand 5 to 10 minutes or until foamy.
2. Stir in remaining sugar, 2 tablespoons butter or margarine, salt and egg until blended. Stir in 1-3/4 cups flour until combined. Stir in enough remaining flour to make a soft dough that comes away from side of bowl.
3. On a lightly floured surface, knead in enough remaining flour to make a stiff dough. Knead 8 to 10 minutes or until smooth and elastic.
4. Clean and grease bowl. Place dough in greased bowl, turning to coat all sides. Cover with a slightly damp towel. Let rise in a warm place, free from drafts, until doubled in bulk, about 1 hour.
5. In a small bowl, combine cinnamon, 1/4 cup sugar, nuts and raisins. Set aside.
6. Grease an 8-inch springform pan or deep cake pan. Punch down dough; cut into 16 equal pieces. Shape each piece into a ball, pinching and tucking sides under. Dip balls in remaining 2 tablespoons melted butter or margarine; roll in sugar-nut mixture. Place 1/2 of coated balls in bottom of greased pan, allowing room for expansion. Place remaining balls on top to make a second layer. Drizzle remaining butter or margarine over top layer; sprinkle with remaining sugar-nut mixture. Cover with a dry towel; let rise until doubled in bulk.
7. Preheat oven to 375F (190C).
8. Bake in preheated oven 30 to 35 minutes or until coffeecake is a deep golden brown and top is firm. Cool in pan on a wire rack 15 minutes. Remove side of pan; slide coffeecake carefully onto rack. Let cool completely.
9. To make icing, in a small bowl, combine powdered sugar and 1 tablespoon milk until smooth and a good pouring consistency, adding more milk if necessary. Drizzle icing over top of coffeecake; let stand until set. Makes 1 coffeecake.

Oatmeal Batter Bread

1 (1/4-oz.) pkg. active dry yeast (1 tablespoon)
1 teaspoon sugar
1 cup warm milk (110F, 45C)
3 tablespoons dark molasses
1/2 cup butter or margarine, room temperature
1-1/2 teaspoons salt
2 eggs
About 3 cups all-purpose flour
1 cup quick-cooking rolled oats
About 2 tablespoons butter or margarine, melted

1. In a large bowl, dissolve yeast and 1 teaspoon sugar in warm milk. Let stand 5 to 10 minutes or until foamy.
2. Add molasses, 1/2 cup butter or margarine, salt, eggs and 1 cup flour to yeast mixture. Beat with an electric mixer on low speed 1 minute or until blended. Increase speed to medium; beat 2 minutes, scraping side of bowl.
3. Add rolled oats and 1-1/2 cups flour. Stir vigorously with a wooden spoon to make a smooth, elastic batter. Stir in enough remaining flour to make a stiff batter that comes away from side of bowl.
4. Cover with a slightly damp towel. Let rise in a warm place, free from drafts, until doubled in bulk, about 1 hour.
5. Grease a 2-quart casserole. Stir down dough with a wooden spoon; scrape into greased casserole with a rubber spatula. Cover with a dry towel; let rise until doubled in bulk.
6. Preheat oven to 375F (190C).
7. Bake in preheated oven 40 to 45 minutes or until top is golden brown and bread sounds hollow when tapped on bottom. Brush top of bread with melted butter or margarine. Remove from casserole; cool completely on a wire rack. Makes 1 loaf.

Left to right: Panettone, Hungarian Coffeecake

Index